FLOATING TO THE FRINGE

On Tour to the Edinburgh Fringe
in an Electric Milk Float

PAUL THOMPSON

First published by Paul Thompson 2020

Copyright © 2020 by Paul Thompson

All rights reserved. No part of this publication may be reproduced, stored or transmitted in any form or by any means, electronic, mechanical, photocopying, recording, scanning, or otherwise without written permission from the publisher. It is illegal to copy this book, post it to a website, or distribute it by any other means without permission.

ISBN: 9798654410399
Print Edition

Cover photo by Chris Taylor
Map designed by Nata Savina

Further information about Paul Thompson,
www.paulsmusic.co.uk

Contents

Dedication	v
Preface	vii
Map	viii
1. Life in the Slow Lane	1
2. Departure Day	11
3. The Milk Float Dimension	20
4. On Top of the Wolds	30
5. To Barnard Castle	42
6. Never Trust a Milkman	53
7. Border Crossing	66
8. Out at Sea	77
9. Arran and Islay	88
10. Colonsay and Oban	100
11. The Outer Hebrides	109
12. Back the Way We Came	120
13. Skye and Rum	130
14. Many Rivers to Cross	139
15. Belladrum	148
16. Ben Nevis and Beyond	161
17. Floating to the Fringe	170
18. Turn It Down Please!	183
19. Homeward Bound	195
About the Author	211

To mum and dad,
for all your love and support

Milk Float (noun)

A slow-moving vehicle, usually with an electric motor, traditionally used for delivering milk to people's doorsteps in the British Isles. In more recent times, a milk float called Bluebell took a different path, delivering music far and wide. This is the story of her journey…

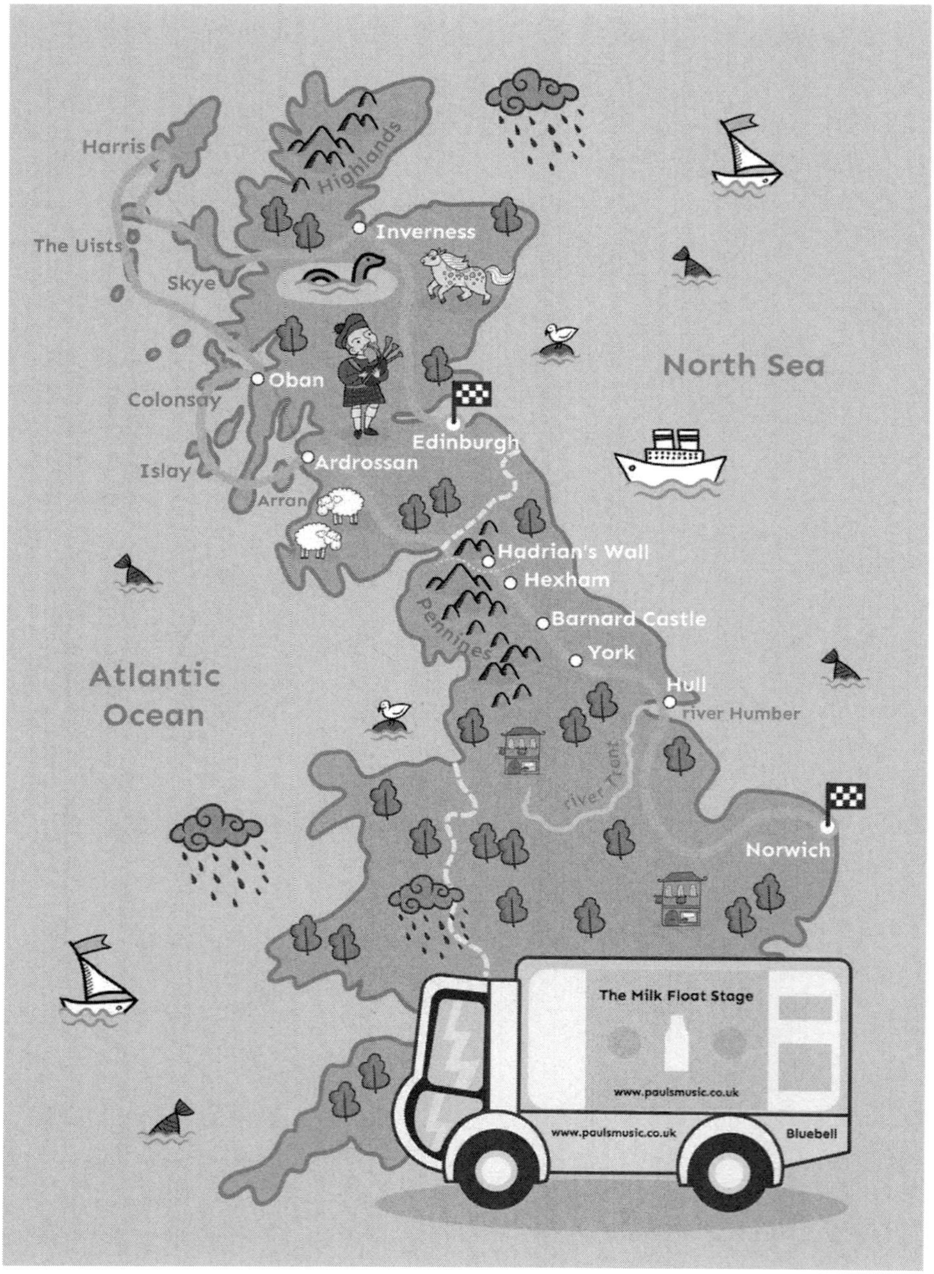
Harris
The Uists
Skye
Highlands
Inverness
Oban
Colonsay
Islay
Arran
Ardrossan
Edinburgh
North Sea
Hadrian's Wall
Hexham
Pennines
Barnard Castle
York
Hull
river Humber
river Trent
Atlantic
Ocean
Norwich
The Milk Float Stage
www.paulsmusic.co.uk
www.paulsmusic.co.uk
Bluebell

ONE

Life in the Slow Lane

IT WAS A sign. Literally. A 'Slow you Down' placard greeting drivers at the start of the small village in North-Norfolk where I live. I'd returned there after completing a degree in Creative Writing, and had been working as a singer-songwriter, as well as doing a care job to help pay the bills. As I stared out of my window one day at the 'Slow You Down' sign during a brain-storming session to think of a tour idea to help promote my next album, for some reason the image of a milk float surfaced in my mind. I was always up for slightly mad-cap adventures to promote my albums, and for the last one had done a tour around Alaska and Canada, hitch-hiking my way through some wild and wonderful places along the way.

Nature is a big inspiration for my songwriting, and I started imagining driving a milk float through the remotest parts of Britain, having time to appreciate its varied landscape away from the hustle of modern life. I knew very little about milk floats except that they were slow, battery powered, and weren't used for delivering milk very much anymore. After doing some research online and posting on milk float forums (yes, they exist!), the general consensus was that it would be almost impossible to do the kind of trip I envisaged in a milk float, partly due to the weight of the batteries, which would also require a huge charger to be carried on-board. The owner of a dairy who'd attempted a road trip for charity in a milk float pessimistically replied to one of my forum posts, 'It will be a bloody miracle if you make it back in one piece'!

There's a stubborn part of me that doesn't like being told that I can't do something. Instead of taking the advice of the 'experts' I tried to think of the most unlikely places you might travel to in Britain by milk float. In a particularly inspired moment, I struck upon the idea of travelling to the Outer Hebrides. It was a place I'd always fancied visiting, which seemed a good enough reason to go! I now needed to find a milk float, and somebody suggested I try a company in Oxfordshire called CBL who specialised in converting milk floats. After speaking on the phone for a while, it seemed that John, the owner, didn't think I was completely insane as I told him about my tour idea. John said that he could fit some special lightweight chargers that I could use to charge the milk float up at campsites, and that if I had a decent set of batteries, the distances I wanted to travel should be achievable.

I arranged to make a visit to John's workshop at Bampton, near Oxford, and turned up one lovely summer's day a few weeks later. The workshop was tucked away down a small alleyway off the main street, with a milk float that looked like a Red Bull can standing at the entrance. John poked his head out from beneath an old-fashioned looking milk float that was in for repairs and a paint job, and came and shook my hand. Everywhere I looked there were milk floats of different shapes and sizes, in various states of decay and repair. There was a really smart milk float with a blue paint job and a catering hatch, and I wondered if this could be the one John had mentioned might be suitable for my tour. My heart fell slightly when I was shown instead a rusty former Madeley Parish Council vehicle that had fallen on hard times, with a punctured tyre, a cab cluttered with rubbish, and a set of dead batteries.

I tried to stay positive, and imagined instead what the milk float would look like once it had been converted. The back wasn't huge, but big enough to fit a small camping bed and some music equipment. It was much lower in height than I'd expected, about four and a half feet high inside, but with a hatch fitted to one side it would be possible to stand beneath to perform outdoors. After taking lots of measurements I went into John's office to discuss prices. The good news was that I could have the milk float for £1,500, but the bad news was that it would cost another £10,000 for a new set of batteries and to do the modifications that I wanted! I told John I'd think about it overnight, and went off to mull things over. I had no idea where I'd get that kind of money from, but I'm a firm believer in following my instincts, and the next day went back to John's workshop and put a £1,000 deposit down, feeling sure that somehow things would work out.

When I got home, I printed a big sign with 'Milk Float HQ' written on it and stuck it to the door of my spare bedroom, which became the centre of milk float tour planning over the next few months. After another long brain-storming session (I was getting good at these!), I came up with the idea of selling advertising space on the milk float. Undeterred by not yet owning a milk float, I printed some leaflets about my tour and started approaching local businesses for sponsorship. I managed to get some good publicity through my local newspaper, the North-Norfolk News, who were highly enthusiastic when I told them about the idea. They fixed up a photo shoot at Dairy Crest in Norwich, and filmed a video of me playing a song from a milk float. I couldn't believe it when my story made it onto the front page of the paper, with the headline 'Local Singer-Songwriter's Milk Float Tour' plastered on billboards outside all the local newsagents.

I had a good relationship with BBC Radio Norfolk, having done several phone-ins for them during my tour of Alaska and Canada, and arranged an interview to go and talk about my latest plans. The first thing that presenter Stephen Bumfrey said to me on-air was, 'Has anybody ever told you that you're completely mad?'!

'I like to think I'm perfectly normal for me,' I quipped back.

Stephen was definitely tickled by my idea, and said that I could pop into the studio whenever I wanted, which would help to keep the project in the public eye. Determined to strike while the iron was hot, I put a box full of leaflets in the back of my car and spent the next week traipsing round all the shops and businesses within a 30-mile radius of my home. Things didn't go as well as I'd hoped as I reeled off my spiel to one shop owner after the other about the benefits of taking out advertising space on my (still non-existent) milk float. Sometimes all that is required to make an idea grow is a small act of faith, and mine came one rainy autumn afternoon, when I phoned Sheringham artist Brian Lewis from Milk Float HQ.

'Yes, I'll take an advert on the milk float,' Brian told me straight away when I explained who I was. I knew Brian vaguely, as he'd bought the hall where my mum had run a children's nursery group, which Brian now used as his studio. My mum had sadly passed away several years earlier, but I felt that somehow she was looking over me, and that it was a good omen that my first sponsor was connected to her. The next day I went to visit Brian, who took me for a spin in his TESLA electric car. When we got back to his studio Brian offered to write me a cheque, and we shook hands on the deal.

It turned out to be a good few days, as I also got my first gig booked for the tour at the Green Britain Centre in Swaffham. Penny, the manager, had been really enthusiastic about the environmentally-friendly element of the tour, as I'd be using solar panels to power my music gear, and generating low carbon-emissions through travelling by battery power. After meeting Penny and being treated to a guided tour to the top of their wind turbine (at the time the only one in Europe with a viewing platform), we set a provisional date for me to perform there at the start of June. Over the coming weeks I gradually gained more sponsors, and started looking into applying for funding from Arts Council England. I'd been in contact with a lady called Helen Meissner who ran an independent record label called Folkstock Records. We met up to discuss her helping to promote the tour, and between us we came up with a plan that we felt might appeal to the Arts Council, offering support slots to up-and-coming singer-songwriters, and running song writing workshops on the days of my gigs.

I'd been working hard on gaining more tour bookings, and now had about 20 provisional dates in England and Scotland. I suddenly realised that I'd be in Scotland around the time of the Edinburgh Fringe, and thought it would be great if I could culminate the tour with some shows there. After making enquiries about places to perform, I was put in touch with a company called Essential Edinburgh, who organised outdoor events on George Street, one of the busiest festival areas. They loved the concept of the milk float, and booked me to play daily for the final two weeks of August. In an inspired moment I decided to call the tour 'Floating to the Fringe'. All I needed now was a milk float!

I put in a huge amount of work into getting my grant application together for Arts Council England, and finally hit the send button on my computer. I now had sponsorship from Roland UK, who were contributing music gear, and I'd also managed to get my ferry tickets paid for by Caledonian MacBrayne, the Scottish ferry company. I'd phoned up the marketing department at CalMac and spoken to a guy called Peter, who turned out to be a total music buff. After talking about music for an hour or so, Peter said he was keen to support the tour, and that I'd need to fill out a sponsorship form on the CalMac website. The next day I had an email back saying that CalMac would be paying for my tickets to travel with the milk float all the way up the west coast of Scotland as far as the Isle of Skye. I couldn't believe my luck!

The Scottish dates were coming together nicely, with bookings to play on the Isle of Arran, Islay (where I'd always wanted to visit because Donovan had written and recorded an album there), Colonsay, the Outer Hebrides, and the Isle of Skye. I also had a booking to play on the Isle of Rum, where vehicles aren't normally allowed due to being a sensitive natural environment. It made my day when a permit came through for me to travel by ferry to Rum, with 'Type of Vehicle – Milk Float!' written on it, and a big warning in red letters saying that there was 'A speed limit of 15mph in Kinloch Village'. I somehow didn't think that would be a problem in my milk float!

I also had several bookings in the Scottish Highlands, thanks to a music promoter called Rob Ellen, who I'd contacted after finding a website he runs for connecting musicians with 'House Concert' hosts. The idea is that somebody with a large enough space in their house to put on a show invites their friends along to watch a touring musician or band play, and at the end of the night everyone donates some money to the band. It's a great way for people to meet with artists on a more personal level, and acts often use it as a means of filling midweek dates that more traditional venues might not book. After a fruitful Skype conversation one afternoon, Rob said he'd send me some more booking contacts and put the word out about my tour.

I was working away when I got a phone call from my dad, who I'd asked to check my post, as I was expecting a decision letter from the Arts Council any day.

'I've got the letter here. Shall I read it for you?' my dad said.

'Go on, then,' I replied.

'I'm sorry to inform you,' he continued, 'but this time your application has been unsuccessful…oh, wait a minute…it says, we're pleased to inform you that your application has been successful.'

I could have strangled my dad for his little joke! After asking him several times, 'So, I've definitely got it then?', I started shouting 'Yes! Yes!', and jumping around my hotel room. So much work had gone into a project that up until that point had still been just a dream, but at last I knew it would become a reality. Admittedly, it was a very strange reality that would involve travelling almost 1,500 miles at 10mph to the furthest reaches of the British Isles, but I was well and truly ready for the challenge.

I'd been keeping John at CBL updated on the progress of my funding application, and organised another visit to his workshop. When I arrived, John said that he'd got another milk float in stock that he thought would be perfect for my tour. It was designed by the engineers at Bluebird, the company that had built the vehicle that set the world land speed record with Donald Campbell. I couldn't help but smile at the irony of a milk float designed by Bluebird, and had a good feeling that this could be my tour vehicle. The milk float was parked at a farm about 10 miles from John's workshop, and one of John's mechanics, Chris, offered to drive me there to view it. I took the opportunity on the way to pick Chris's brains about the potential downfalls of travelling the country in a milk float.

'Not a lot can go wrong except for the motor burning out…oh, and they can catch alight if you travel downhill too quickly and the motor sticks,' he said cheerfully.

As soon as the Bluebird milk float came into view, I knew it was the one for me. Bigger than an average-sized milk float, it had a modern, almost futuristic design, with lovely curved glass doors, retro wheel-arches, and a long back section that would be perfect for converting into a living / performance space. Chris said I could take the milk float for a test-drive, and I felt quite nervous as I turned the ignition key and heard the motor whirring into life. There was a small green button between the seats that you had to push downwards to engage forward motion, or press upwards for reverse, which triggered a loud reversing alarm.

As I put my foot down on the accelerator for the first time, I was surprised at how quickly the float pulled away. I drove to the end of the farm track and a short distance up the road, feeling like a small child in an over-sized dodgem. There were only two foot-pedals, one for accelerating and the other for braking. Turning round was quite tricky as there was no rear-view mirror, and I had to rely instead on the large wing-mirrors. Luckily there was no traffic about to witness my 7-point turn, although the farmer whose yard John was using seemed to find my maiden voyage quite amusing.

'Do you want to buy a horse instead?' he joked as I returned to the yard.

I tried not to show Chris how keen I was on the float as we drove back to CBL to discuss prices. John said the Bluebird milk float was going to cost a lot more than the first one I'd put a deposit on, but if the batteries were ok, it would still work out about the same overall. We eventually settled on a price that would include all the conversion work, plus fitting some leisure batteries and an inverter that I could wire solar-panels into for powering my music equipment.

I still had a huge amount to do before I left on tour. My album needed the final mixes doing, the covers designing, and the CDs printed. I had tour posters to design and print, and they needed sending out to the venues. I was also negotiating booking terms with many of the venues and trying to fill in gaps in my schedule, which meant phone calls and emails to constantly chase-up, and I still hadn't worked out where I'd be staying in between gigs. I'd advertised support-slots for the tour on the Arts Council jobs website, and had hundreds of replies to wade through.

Eventually I short-listed the acts whose music I liked, and that I felt would fit best with the ethos of the tour. I also had a couple of artists from Folkstock Records playing some dates, and had met with one of them, Daria Kulesh, a Russian singer-songwriter now living in England. Daria was really keen on playing some dates in the Isle of Skye, but I only had funding from the Arts Council for the English part of the tour. I agreed to guarantee Daria a few support slots on Skye, and also offered all the acts who were playing in England the chance to come and perform in Edinburgh.

It was around this time that my dad received the devastating news that he'd got cancer. We didn't know if he'd have to undergo chemotherapy, and I seriously considered putting a halt to the tour, as he'd need a lot of support during the months ahead. Luckily, I have two caring brothers who offered to help out as much as they could, and I was touched that my whole family, including my dad, insisted that I do the tour no matter what happened.

TWO

Departure Day

THE MORNING THE milk float was due to arrive I woke up feeling like an excited child on my birthday. John had organised for the float to be delivered on the back of a trailer, and I stood eagerly waiting in the middle of the village street with my video camera, ready to capture the moment it appeared around the corner. Eventually I heard the rumbling of wheels, and guessed this must be it. The milk float looked amazing on the back of the trailer with its new makeover. It now had an enclosed back section, with windows on one side and a big metal catering hatch on the other. It didn't take long for the driver to reverse the float off the trailer, and after making him a cup of tea before he started the long journey back to Oxfordshire, I was left standing with the keys wondering what to do next. There was only one thing for it – go for a spin!

There wasn't much traffic about as I bumped along past farms and cottages on the way to the next village, where I turned off onto a narrow road that followed the edge of a wood. All seemed to be going well until I noticed the level of the battery meter. It had dropped from full to almost empty in just over three miles. I phoned John at CBL, who said that because the milk float had been standing for so long, I would need to cycle the batteries by giving them gradually longer runs to give them a chance to build strength again. He assured me that all was not lost, and that I would just have to see how things went over the next week or so before making a decision about replacing the batteries.

After posting some pictures on Facebook with the caption 'Introducing the milk float made by Bluebird', one of my friends replied saying how much they liked 'Bluebell'. I still needed to find a name for my new milk float, which by a strange coincidence was parked in my garden next to a clump of bluebells. I decided that the float would be called 'Bluebell', thinking that it also sounded like the kind of name you might give a to a cow!

I had my first booking with Bluebell the following week in Cromer, about 10 miles from where I lived, but I was still unsure of whether the batteries were strong enough to get me there. I phoned a guy called Rory, who lived near the Norfolk broads, and had replied to one of my posts on a milk float forum. I'd visited Rory a few months earlier, and he'd shown me his collection of electric vehicles, including a dilapidated milk float that he'd used to commute to work with. Rory was a bit of an eccentric, a trained engineer and electric vehicle enthusiast, and he kindly offered to come over and do some tests on Bluebell's batteries.

We lifted the floor boards in the back section of the float, revealing two sets of huge battery packs with 18 cells in each. Rory methodically numbered all the cells and made some voltage readings, muttering incomprehensible equations as he went. After driving to the next village and back, Rory took another battery reading and said, 'That's a really good sign. The voltage levels have barely dropped.'

Rory suggested that I do a longer run to see how far I could get, so the next morning I woke up early, made a flask of tea and set off through the Norfolk countryside, singing as I went. It was a beautiful May morning, and after reaching the nearest town of Holt, I turned off towards the coast road and soon had fantastic views out to sea. The height of the cab meant that I could see much more than I would from a car, and the wide screen provided a panoramic view of my surroundings. I stopped at the little coastal village of Blakeney, and sat in the cab drinking tea and looking out at the boats, feeling glad to be alive.

By the time I got home I calculated that I'd done about 20 miles, which would be easily enough to get me to my gig at Cromer that weekend. I'd been booked to play outside the pier for the annual 'Crab and Lobster Festival', and had a reporter coming from the North-Norfolk News to interview me and take photos. There was still a lot of work to do to get Bluebell fitted out, and I had a list of jobs as long as my arm to wade through.

I spent the rest of the day cutting and fitting a carpet and putting curtains up. The solar panels were proving to be more difficult to install. I knew virtually nothing about solar power prior to the project, and had learnt what I did know from the internet. I'd bought two lightweight flexible solar-panels that were designed to be glued onto outdoor surfaces, but the roof of the milk float was made of fibre-glass, and had warped slightly, which meant the panels didn't have a flat surface to stick to. I came up with the idea of laying flagstones on top of the solar panels so that they'd be forced to stick, and to my amazement it worked perfectly. The only problem now was that there was no power getting through from the panels to the leisure batteries!

As would happen so many times during my tour, a small twist of fate was waiting to help me out in my time of need. I drove Bluebell later that day into Sheringham to visit my dad, and we'd just returned from walking his dog when a man came down my dad's drive carrying some leaflets. Noticing that he was advertising as an electrician, I asked him if he knew anything about solar panels.

'I certainly do,' he replied, and went to fetch his work van.

Clive was soon up a ladder testing all my connections on the solar panels, and it didn't take him long to discover that one of the connectors between the solar panels and the inverter was faulty. After replacing the connector, Clive switched the circuit breaker on, and the control panel showed a healthy 48 volts flowing into the inverter. The show could now officially go on!

It was an exciting feeling packing Bluebell ready for my first gig the following Saturday at Cromer Pier. I drove across country to Cromer, and as I came into the town centre, I noticed people were stopping to look at the float. I had to negotiate a steep fisherman's ramp to get down onto the promenade, and was soon parked in front of the pier with a small crowd gathered round. After doing an interview for the North-Norfolk News, I started playing some songs, and not long after was joined by two figures in giant crab and lobster costumes dancing along to the music. I have to say it was one of the most surreal moments of my life!

I had an evening gig to get to on a playing field just out of town, and after packing my music gear up, I attempted to drive back up the fisherman's slope. Bluebell slowed down as I drove up the steep cobbled incline, eventually grinding to a halt about halfway up. This was not good. If I couldn't even get up a small slope, how on earth was I going to get all the way to the Outer Hebrides? Fortunately for me there was a more gradual slope at the other end of the promenade, and in what was to become a regular mantra during my trip, I shouted, 'Come on Bluebell, you can do it!' as we wound our way to the top.

The final week before departure was a mad scramble to get everything ready in time. I had the sponsors' adverts fitted to Bluebell by a local sign-writer, and the float looked fantastic with my tour logo in the centre of the catering hatch, and 'Floating to the Fringe' written in huge letters above. My cottage was a complete mess of CDs, posters, music and camping equipment, all waiting to be packed into the float, and I still had to get the place ready for some tenants who were moving in for the summer.

I wanted to do a longer test-run to see if the batteries were capable of the 35 to 40 mile distances I needed to be able to cover each day for the tour, and set off one afternoon for Wells-Next-the-Sea, which I worked out was a 38 mile round-trip. The coast road was busy with holiday-makers, and at one point I pulled over and counted more than 30 cars overtaking me. I'd had an extra window fitted so that I could see out of the back of Bluebell from the cab, but as I watched some of the irate drivers stuck behind me, I wondered if I would have been better off without it!

When I reached Wells-Next-the-Sea I did a voltmeter test that showed the batteries hadn't dropped too much, and after an ice cream and a wander along the quay I headed for home. Bluebell slowed down for the last few miles, but despite the battery indicator flashing empty, we made it safely back to my cottage. It was brilliant news, and for the first time I felt confident that Bluebell might actually be able to complete the tour.

Two days before leaving, I had my album launch at a beautiful nature reserve on the North-Norfolk coast called Cley Marshes. I was running a song-writing workshop in the afternoon, and there was just enough time afterwards to set up for the evening performance. A fantastic singer-songwriter called Kelly Oliver was opening for me, who Helen Meissner from Folkstock Records had driven all the way from Hertfordshire. It was a magical night, and a flock of geese flew by with the setting sun behind me, just as I was playing a song called 'Flights of Geese' from my new album.

The day before leaving was spent loading Bluebell up ready for three months on the road. Every possible space was crammed full of guitars, amps, clothes, food and cooking equipment. Charging cables were stuffed behind seats in the front cab, my duvet strapped into the driver's seat, and storage containers piled up in the back. I also had a huge container of de-ionised water in the front cab, which I'd need for filling up the batteries along the way. My dad came over early the next morning to help with some last-minute jobs, and we said an emotional farewell, choking back tears as we gave each other a big hug.

Finally, the moment of no return had arrived. I sat in Bluebell, drew a deep breath, switched on the ignition and pulled away. I was due in Norwich by 2pm, where Radio Norfolk would be doing a live send-off outside the BBC studios. I was starting to get used to Bluebell's natural pace, which on a flat road was about 18mph. Going downhill, she could get up to almost 30mph, but anything beyond that and the cab started violently rattling! Uphill was a different story, and depending on how steep the hill was, we would slow down to about 5mph.

It was the first time I'd done any city driving with Bluebell, but she fitted in perfectly with the flow of traffic, which was fairly slow-moving anyway. As I approached the ring road in Norwich, several cars started hooting and waving at me, I think in a friendly way! The producer of Radio Norfolk, Thordis, was waiting for me outside the BBC studios when I arrived, and said she'd be doing the interview, as it was Stephen Bumfrey's day off. Thordis was just as enthusiastic about my tour as Stephen had been.

'We'll do the interview inside the milk float,' Thordis said, 'and then you can play a song for us.'

I got my music gear set up and played a few songs before Thordis came back out holding a microphone, ready for us to go live on-air. The interview went really well as I described to the listeners what Bluebell looked like.

'I never expected it to be so modern-looking…it's brilliant!' enthused Thordis.

I suddenly felt a surge of pride at what I'd achieved in getting this far. Bluebell was graceful and unique, with a real personality of her own. Even if I didn't make it all the way to Edinburgh, I'd still have surpassed many people's expectations, and there were quite a few people who didn't even think I'd make it out of Norfolk. I was determined to prove them wrong.

I was booked to stay the night at a campsite just outside Norwich, where my brother, Andy, had arranged for us to have a Chinese meal delivered. I still hadn't quite got the hang of my new satnav, and almost ended up on the A11. After pulling into a petrol station to ask directions, I eventually found my turning and was greeted by a friendly couple who ran the campsite. Once I'd parked up and got Bluebell on charge, I was soon surrounded by inquisitive campers. It would be the first of an endless amount of times on my trip that I was asked the questions, 'So what's the top speed?' and, 'How many miles can it go on a charge?' A friend had suggested a few weeks earlier that I should get a T-shirt made with '15mph, 30 miles per day' written on it, and it was advice I would come to wish I'd taken!

When the Chinese arrived, Andy and I crammed into the back of Bluebell and I fetched us some plates and cutlery out. It was an odd feeling eating a meal in the back of a milk float, sitting looking out of the hatch at the campers coming and going. This was the first time I'd stopped all day, and I suddenly realised how exhausted I was. After a brotherly hug, Andy and I said our farewells and I prepared for my first night sleeping in Bluebell. I had a small sofa bed that pulled out and needed making up. Beneath a window at the back of the float, there was a small wooden chest with my cooking utensils in, where I would place a reading lamp at night. I'd not yet managed to get my small TV working, but I was so tired after my long day that after reading a few pages of my book I was sound asleep, dreaming of the adventures that lay ahead.

THREE

The Milk Float Dimension

IT TOOK ME a while the next morning to get into my new routine. I had to lie down to get dressed as the roof of the milk float was so low, and several expletives later I emerged with my clothes on. I'd packed an old camping kettle that fell apart when I tried brewing up my first cup of tea – this was a situation that would need urgent attention! My most important job each morning was to check that the batteries had charged up overnight. I had two chargers fitted in the front cab that could be connected to camp site hook-ups, and a dial on the dashboard flashed red, amber and finally green when each of the batteries was fully charged. It took eight hours for a full charge, and it made me ridiculously happy to see both dials flashing green in preparation for my journey that day, which would take me to Ashill, near Swaffham, where I had a gig at the Green Britain Centre the following day.

I had another reason for staying at Ashill, as I'd worked there for a while with my care job, looking after a man who had multiple sclerosis. An elderly neighbour, Lillian, who used to come and help me, had kindly offered to cook me a meal that night, an offer too good to refuse as I remembered the lovely cakes Lillian used to bring me at work. After telling a few more of the campers about my trip (yep, 15mph, 30 miles per day!), I was soon out of Norwich and on my way to Ashill. I had all day to get there, and kept stopping along the way to pose for photos with Bluebell. When I reached the town of Watton I went in search of a new kettle, and as luck would have it also managed to find a TV aerial shop.

I explained to the shop owner about needing an aerial for the milk float (now it's not every day you get a request like that!), and he showed me a huge aerial which he said should give me a decent signal in most parts of the country. He cut some wiring for it and only charged me £10, which I thought was a bargain. I'd managed to find a lovely little dark blue whistling kettle for £7, and returned to Bluebell feeling very pleased with my purchases.

After finding my camp site at Ashill, I attempted some re-organising in the back of Bluebell, as things were getting untidy very quickly. I spent the afternoon pulling boxes out and trying to fit them back in different ways, but whatever I tried didn't seem to make much difference. It didn't occur to me that perhaps the problem was that I'd brought too much stuff with me! By the time Lillian's partner, Barry, arrived to pick me up I was feeling hot and bothered from moving everything around, and was in even more of a mess than when I'd started.

'I'm just having a bit of a sort out,' I explained to Barry, who found the whole thing highly amusing.

'Well, we'd better not keep Lillian waiting too long, she's been baking all afternoon,' he replied.

Abandoning my efforts at tidying up, we left Bluebell on

charge and drove in Barry's car to Ashill. Lillian gave me a big kiss, and I could smell delicious home cooking coming from the kitchen. Soon, plate after plate was being brought out onto the dining table, stacked with steamed and roast vegetables, olives, garlic bread and a huge roast chicken. I'd already eaten far too much by the time pudding was served, homemade apple pie with cream.

'I've got something else for you, too,' said Lillian, producing a massive sponge cake for me to take back to the milk float with me.

I was touched by Lillian being so motherly, and she said to make sure I kept in touch. By the time I got back to Bluebell I was too tired to do any more tidying, and spent an hour looking through some workshop materials for the next day, when I'd be teaching a group of 20 schoolchildren songwriting from the top of a wind turbine.

I was up early the next morning as I needed to be at the Green Britain Centre by 9am, ready for the children arriving. It was only about six miles to Swaffham, but the road weaved and turned all the way making it difficult for traffic to overtake, and I had a long queue behind me as we rolled into town. I took a photo of Bluebell beneath the wind turbine at the entrance to the Green Britain Centre, and she looked really comical dwarfed by the giant arms of the turbine above her. It was Penny the manager's day off, and I was greeted instead by the assistant manager, Paul, who'd been helping to do some publicity for the event.

It wasn't long before the schoolchildren arrived, and after a short introduction I led the way up the spiral staircase of the wind turbine. The children's footsteps and excited voices echoed around the huge cylinder as we climbed higher, the turbine occasionally swaying in the breeze. The scenery from the top was spectacular, with a circular platform giving probably the best panoramic views to be found anywhere in Norfolk, looking across miles of farmland and woods towards the sea.

After explaining to the children about how we can use the senses to write song lyrics, I asked them to write down descriptions of the things they could see from the viewing tower. I'd thought it would inspire them to write beautiful song lyrics, but for some reason they were finding it more difficult than I'd expected. The boys especially didn't have very much written down when I walked around ten minutes later to see how they were doing. I tried prompting them by asking them to tell me what they could see, which unfortunately resulted in 'supermarket,' 'cars', and one boy had spotted a portaloo in a farmer's field!

I was hoping things would go better in the second half of the workshop, when we returned to the conference room in the Green Britain Centre. I'd planned to ask the children to think of some song titles based around their observations, but 'The Swaffham Portaloo' probably wouldn't have made the best of song titles! I asked them to use their imaginations instead, and they soon started coming up with some good ideas. After separating into groups, they read their song lyrics out loud, and the results were fantastic.

Once the children had left, I went in search of my camp site as it would be late in the evening by the time my gig finished, and I wanted to make sure I'd be able to get Bluebell on charge overnight. Breckland Meadows was only about a mile out of the town centre, and I was greeted by a friendly camp site owner who pointed me in the direction of my pitch. I just had time for a late lunch and a short nap before heading back to the Green Britain Centre to get set up for the evening event.

Paul helped me reverse Bluebell up to some wide doors that opened into the restaurant area where I'd be performing, and with a bit of manoeuvring we were able to open Bluebell's hatch so that it was inside the room. I had two support acts playing, a young vocal harmony group called 'Vibe', and a singer-songwriter called Steve Young. I already knew Zoe, one of the members of Vibe, who I'd done some recording for with her previous band, and she'd also sung backing vocals on my latest album. Steve Young had replied to my advert for support slots on the Arts Council website, and I'd liked his music which was well-written and arranged, and he had a great CV, having worked with people like Lionel Richie as a session guitarist.

It took over two hours to get sound-checked, and after doing an interview with a journalist from a local magazine, I barely had time to get changed before the audience started arriving. The gig had been well publicised, but I had no idea how many people to expect as it was the first time the Green Britain Centre had put on a live music event. Vibe and Steve Young had brought along their friends and family, so at least I knew we had a guaranteed audience. Vibe kicked off the evening performing soulful three-part harmonies accompanied by a fantastic young guitarist. I took the opportunity to quickly eat a vegetable lasagne before introducing Steve Young, and realised afterwards I'd spilt half of the lasagne down my clean white shirt! Food spillages aside, the audience was very appreciative, and we all sold some CDs at the end of the night which is always a bonus. Steve would be joining me again at Far Ings, a nature reserve near the banks of the river Humber, where I'd be playing the following Friday. After packing my music gear away, Paul helped me reverse Bluebell out of the restaurant, and I drove back to the camp site for a well-earned rest.

During my usual inspection of the battery chargers the next morning I noticed that one of the cables had tripped during the night, which was bad news as it would mean waiting around for the battery to finish charging before I could set off. I suspected one of my charging cables might be faulty, and went to see if the campsite owner had any for sale.

'I don't, but I know a man who does,' he said, and took me to a caravan a few pitches down from mine to introduce me to Richard, an ex-electrician who'd taken early retirement and was staying on-site. Richard offered to make up another cable for me, and said it could be ready in an hour. I ate my breakfast in the back of Bluebell, looking at my huge map and trying to work out a quiet route to my next destination, a campsite called 'The Secret Garden' just outside Wisbech. When I'd spoken to one of the owners, Lesley, she'd said they were full, but after I explained about the milk float tour she thought I'd be perfect accompaniment for their beer and sausage tasting event that was happening that Saturday night, and said she'd find a way to fit myself and Bluebell in.

As promised, Richard returned an hour later with my cable, and it wasn't long before Bluebell's charger was flashing green. I had 31 miles to cover that day, the furthest distance of the tour so far. As I drove along a quiet country lane around the edge of Thetford Forest, I felt an overwhelming surge of joy at being on my adventure. I still hadn't got used to the surrealness of travelling by milk float, and it was a very weird feeling thinking that I'd be continuing at this pace all the way to Scotland. I named it the Milk Float Dimension!

After following a backroad into the town of Downham Market, I stopped for supplies before taking a busier A-road towards Wisbech. Despite a long line of over-taking cars, it was a pretty route that followed a canal for several miles with brightly painted houseboats moored along its banks. The satnav guided Bluebell around Wisbech and back out into the Cambridgeshire Fens, officially crossing our first county border! When I turned into the small lane that led to the Secret Garden, Neil, Lesley's husband, was standing at the gates with a big grin on his face.

'You must be Paul' he said, offering me his hand to shake.

'And you must be psychic,' I replied, although I think it was more to do with the fact that I was travelling in a milk float that had my name plastered all over it!

Neil gave me a guided tour of the brewery they had on-site, and showed me a lovely wildlife area they'd been developing for the campers to enjoy. After getting Bluebell parked next to the marquee where I'd be performing that night, we unreeled my cables to a power-point in a huge poly-tunnel so that I could get the batteries on charge. It didn't take long to set my music gear up for the beer and sausage tasting event, and there was a nice communal feel to the evening with families sharing the barbecue area. I was treated to several hot-dogs, kebabs and chicken-wings in between songs, and Neil and Lesley asked if I'd mind having a photo taken with Bluebell for their local paper. I was soon surrounded by Neil and Lesley's family and friends holding up bottles of locally brewed beer for the camera. I was starting to feel much more relaxed now that the stress of preparing for the tour was over.

I had a short journey planned the next day, to the aptly named Bluebell Inn at Whaplode St. Catherine, about 16 miles away. It was warm and sunny when I set off, crossing almost immediately into the Lincolnshire Fens. This was the classic flatlands that people imagine when they think of Lincolnshire, a maze of small lanes that follow dykes for miles on end, with huge skies that make for an artist's paradise. 'Fen' is the East Anglian name for marshland, a vast wetland that lies mainly at sea level, and spreads across Lincolnshire, Cambridgeshire, Huntingdonshire, Norfolk and Suffolk, covering almost 1,500 square miles.

I finally worked out that if I set my satnav for 'Shortest Distance', it would naturally take me off the busy roads and go the most direct route instead, which suited me fine. I meandered past miles of farmland with barely a house in sight, enjoying the views of corn swaying in the breeze, and the occasional bird following Bluebell's happy trail. In some ways the Fens reminded me of the American mid-west, and I started imagining myself in a kind of Fenland Hitchcock film, with Bluebell breaking down on a crossroads somewhere, and having to hitch a lift on the back of a pick-up truck to the nearest town, where I'd meet a grizzly end at the local motel!

Luckily, the satnav guided me to the Bluebell Inn instead, a quaint country pub with a small campsite attached. After a leisurely siesta I spent the afternoon fitting my TV aerial, drilling holes into the side of Bluebell so that I could attach the bracket. To my amazement I soon had a perfect TV reception, and celebrated with a cup of tea and cake. Several campers came over during the afternoon to have a look at Bluebell and take photos. I was running a competition to win a free download each week of my album, and to enter people had to share a photo of Bluebell on social media with a funny caption. I was hoping that the competition would help raise publicity for the tour, and I had Helen Meissner from Folkstock records also doing PR for me, organising interviews with regional newspapers and BBC radio stations on my route.

I had a long journey planned the next day to a place called Tattershall Lakes, where I was booked in at a large caravan park. I left about mid-day, following a quiet B-road into Spalding, a pretty town with the River Welland flowing through its centre. The wind was ferocious and slowed Bluebell down by at least 3-4mph, which may not sound like a lot, but when you can only travel at 15mph believe me every little bit helps!

The wind was also taking its toll on the batteries, which were flashing red after only about 20 miles. I stopped to give Bluebell a rest at the small town of Kirton, and then took a single-track road that followed a dyke called Holland Fen for about six miles. I was driving into a fierce crosswind that was blowing Bluebell about on the road, and I anxiously watched the battery meter flashing an amber warning light with an exclamation mark. No manual had come with the float, and I had no idea what all the different symbols on the dashboard meant. There was a little spanner sign that would appear every now and then, which didn't look too promising either. Bluebell eventually crawled into Tattershall Lakes Caravan Park, and just made it to her pitch for the night.

I spent the evening poring over my map, trying to work out my route for the next few days. I'd never been to the Lincolnshire Wolds before, which I'd heard were beautiful, and I plotted a course that would take me right through the middle of them, bringing me out the other side near Humber airport. I was also using a website to help plot my routes that showed the gradients of the hills, and despite people telling me that Lincolnshire was flat, some of the hills I'd be crossing in the Wolds looked extremely steep. I just hoped that Bluebell would be up to the challenge.

FOUR

On Top of the Wolds

THE WIND HAD dropped by the next morning, and with Bluebell's batteries fully charged I set off towards the market town of Woodhall Spa, stopping for some supplies and a wander round its quiet streets. I'd planned on having a fairly easy day, but as we were making good progress, I decided to head for a campsite in the middle of the Lincolnshire Wolds, at a village called Binbrook. Woodhall Spa marked the transition between the Fenlands and the Wolds, and I was soon out into beautiful rolling countryside that reminded me more of parts of Yorkshire or Devon.

After crossing a main road at Horncastle, the hills became even bigger, and Bluebell finally met her match at a place called Scramblesby. The hill ahead was so big I could barely see the summit, and a warning sign at the bottom had '10% Gradient' ominously written on it. I cursed myself for not having planned my route more carefully, and considered turning round, but Bluebell had already crossed several big hills, and the batteries were starting to get low.

There was only one thing to do – put my foot down on the accelerator and hope for the best! My senses were finely tuned to every nuance of the motor as we gradually climbed higher. By halfway there was an alarming smell of burning, and we'd slowed to 3mph as the hill reached the steepest section. The occasional car would overtake, looking inquisitively at me as I shouted, 'Come on Bluebell, you can do it!' We were only 50 yards from the top of the hill when Bluebell's motor finally gave up, and ground to a halt.

I jammed on the brake, and after a long five minutes I turned the ignition back on and we just managed to crawl the final few yards to the top of the hill. I didn't know if I'd damaged the motor, and phoned John from CBL to ask his advice. He told me to check the motor, which was red hot when I touched it. John said to give the motor an hour or so to cool down and then see if it would run again. I was parked only half a mile from Cadwell Park racing circuit, and I couldn't help smile at the irony of my situation, with the sound of racing cars whizzing round a track at 150mph. Talk about life in the fast lane compared to the slow! I did the only sensible thing one could do in such a situation. I put the kettle on and made a nice cup of tea while I tried to figure out what to do next.

It was still another 15 miles to my campsite, and it was too far to go back the way I'd come. After an hour or so, I switched the ignition back on and drove a short way up the road. Bluebell appeared to be driving normally again, and I decided to continue towards Binbrook. We were now on a plateau that took us directly through the centre of the Wolds, and it was an incredibly beautiful drive past miles of farmland, with cows grazing peacefully in summer fields.

After climbing another couple of steep hills we finally made it to our campsite, Hopeville Farm. There was no sign of anybody at the farmhouse, except for a dog barking excitedly at the letter box. It was a scruffy looking place, with rubbish piled in the barns and a dilapidated shipping container with 'toilets' scrawled on a sign above it. The view across the Wolds was incredible, though, and after sitting for a while looking out of Bluebell at the wooded valley, a man turned up who was staying on the camp site, and said that the farmer would be along later.

I moved Bluebell onto the camping field and gave John from CBL a ring to let him know I'd arrived safely. He didn't think that I'd permanently damaged the motor, and said Bluebell should be ok to carry on. With most of the afternoon still ahead of me, I took the opportunity to re-fill the batteries, which was quite a task. First, I had to remove everything from inside the milk float so that I could lift the carpet to get to the batteries. With guitars, amplifiers and a sofa lying on the field, I then had to remove the floorboards, and using a funnel, pour water into each of the 36 battery cells. It was the first time I'd topped the batteries up, and I was amazed at how much water they'd used. In the end it took almost a whole 50 litre container of de-ionised water to re-fill them.

I was just finishing off when the farmer turned up, who was very friendly despite me having arrived unannounced and put half the contents of Bluebell onto his field. After cooking supper, I walked to the farmhouse to ask the farmer the best way to go the next day, and was accosted by his dog, a small Jack-Russell who grabbed onto my boot and wouldn't let go. It must have looked quite comical as I tried climbing over the farmer's gate, shaking my leg and shouting, 'Get off you stupid dog!' Eventually the dog dropped to the other side, and I abandoned my quest, retreating to the safety of Bluebell. I suddenly felt very alone as I reflected on the day I'd had. I'd been on the road for exactly a week, and had already come close to burning Bluebell's motor out. We'd covered 173 miles, and still had over a thousand to go, with the hilliest sections yet to come. It was going to be a long trip!

I woke up the next morning feeling much more positive, and after an early breakfast and check of the batteries I was on the road again. I didn't have far to travel that day, about 18 miles to a farm with a campsite on it, just the other side of the Wolds. After the near breakdown the day before I didn't want to take any chances, and phoned ahead to ask which would be the flattest way to go. I spoke with the farmer, Peter, who said I could take a detour past Humber Airport that would bring me into the village of Barnetby Le Wold, avoiding any steep hills.

Despite their beauty, I was glad to see the back of the Wolds as I drove steadily into a flatter landscape. After passing the airport I turned down a road that I thought would lead me towards the campsite, but it turned out to be a potholed track with a couple of cottages at the end. I'd stopped to look at my map when a lady came out and asked if I needed any help.

'Yes,' I wanted to reply, 'I'm driving to Scotland in a milk float, I think I need a good psychiatrist!'.

I explained where I was trying to get to, and the lady called her husband, who then started arguing with her about which was the best road to go on. They eventually decided that I needed to go back the way I'd come, and take the next but one left hand turning (the first would bring me onto Runway One of Humber Airport, so best avoided!). I thanked them, and left them arguing as Bluebell bumped back over the potholes to the main road. After driving for another mile or so with a huge tailback of traffic, I was glad to get off the main road as we followed a pretty country lane to the camp site.

Peter and his wife were a lovely couple, and when I told them about my tour, Peter said that he wouldn't charge me to stay for the night. Wold Farm was just what I needed after the stress of the previous day. Positioned at the top of a wide valley, it had lovely views across woodland, and the occasional light aircraft would pass on its way in and out of Humber airport. Peter's wife offered to do my washing for me when I asked if there was a laundrette, and she even brought me some supplies that I needed from the local shop. I sat for the afternoon on my little camping chair watching swallows come and go, and after a stroll through some barley fields, cooked a fish stew, eating it looking out at the sunset.

I was due at Far Ings Nature Reserve in a couple of days for my next gig, and had made good progress, being only about 20 miles away. I booked into a campsite the next day in a place called New Holland, on the eastern banks of the Humber, that was also home to a herd of alpacas. From Wold Farm, I followed a tiny road all the way to Barton-Upon-Humber with barely a car in site, stopping in the town for a look round. Every now and then I'd glimpse the Humber Bridge, which looked imposing and impressive, and I felt a twinge of nerves at the thought of crossing it on Saturday.

After following a main road out of town, I turned off towards New Holland. As early as the 14th Century a ferry had been taking passengers from Barton across to Hull, and it ran until the 1850s, superseded by a ferry from New Holland that ran until 1981, when the Humber Bridge was opened. My campsite for the night, 'Marshland Alpacas', was down a single track at the end of the town. Julie and Gary, the owners, were very friendly, and guided me through a gate into the camping field, which was next to a field full of alpacas. Julie told me about her alpaca business, selling fleece which is used to make clothing and extremely comfortable mattresses, duvets and pillows. I spent the rest of the day catching up on tour emails and playing guitar, as the alpacas stood with their long necks above the fence inquisitively watching me.

After giving Bluebell a good wash the next morning, I left for Far Ings nature reserve, where I was due to be running a songwriting workshop ahead of my evening gig. When I reached Barton, I stopped at my campsite to check-in, and afterwards found a Tesco to re-stock on supplies. When I went to pay at the till, I suddenly had a complete mental blank and couldn't remember the pin number for my bank card. After three attempts my card was blocked, and I had to phone my bank up to get it sorted. I realised what had happened – my forgetfulness was a result of being in the Milk Float Dimension. Gradually the trappings of modern-day living were becoming less important, and it was starting to affect my ability to function in the normal world!

Finally escaping the Tesco car park, I followed a long single-track road running parallel with the banks of the River Humber. Far Ings Nature Reserve is home to, amongst other things, migrating geese, swifts, swallows, wading birds and bitterns, and as a bonus has a spectacular view of the Humber Bridge. I'd been in touch with Leanne, the manager, for several months, who was originally from Norfolk, and was very enthusiastic about the milk float tour. Leanne said that she was expecting quite a few people in the evening, but wasn't sure if many would turn up for the workshop, as only one couple had booked so far.

After being given a guided tour of the centre, I fetched the workshop materials out of Bluebell and waited for people to arrive. By about 2.30pm there was no sign of anybody, and Leanne apologetically told me that the she'd had an email from the couple saying that they couldn't make it that afternoon, but would be along for the evening gig. Leanne and the other centre manager, Susan, were busy sectioning off a grassy area that contained some rare bee orchids, and I offered to give them a hand.

I spent a nice afternoon exploring the reserve, and it was soon time to start loading my music gear in for the evening gig. Steve Young turned up just as I was finishing setting up, and after doing a sound-check we had a chance to chat and get to know each other better. Leanne had ordered some pizza for us all, and we sat outside sharing food. I got chatting to an elderly volunteer who said, 'My brother-in-law's a folk singer. His name's Martin Simpson, do you know him?', I couldn't believe it – one of the biggest folk names in the country! I gave the lady a CD and leaflet about the tour for her to pass on to him. It just shows – it pays to be friendly to everyone!

There was a friendly crowd along for the evening gig, with

a lovely backdrop of reed beds and the Humber Bridge behind me as I played. It was almost midnight by the time I left, and it felt very surreal driving back along the dark single-track road towards the town, with the Humber Bridge lit up, and the only sound coming from the hum of Bluebell's motor. I managed to get lost in the deserted streets of Barton, and stopped to ask directions from a man who was walking his dog. He looked absolutely terrified as Bluebell drew alongside him.

'It's a milk float,' I explained, which seemed to scare the poor man even more.

After finally finding the campsite and getting Bluebell on charge, I ate some supper and sat watching TV for a while. In my younger days I would have gone in search of a late-night bar, but I'd given up drinking a few years previously, and had no desire anymore to punish my body with hangovers. As I like to tell people now, 'I'm ex drugs, but still rock and roll!'

I was awake bright and early the next morning, ready for a live telephone interview with BBC Radio Humber. I had my longest day of travel so far, across the Humber Bridge to a backpacker hostel called Naburn Station just below York, 41 miles away. The toilet facilities at my camp site were the worst of my tour so far, with a plastic portaloo that barely had room to stand up in, and no hand basin. I had to use an outside tap to brush my teeth, and shaved with the help of one of Bluebell's wing-mirrors so that I could see what I was doing. Camping is definitely all about the art of improvisation!

I'd learnt from previous tours that it's a good idea to jot a few points down ahead of a live radio interview, as you never know how long you've got on-air, and it's important to get any information across such as gig dates as quickly as possible. The first time I'd done a radio phone-in was from Alaska with Stephen Bumfrey on Radio Norfolk. Because of the time difference, I had to get up at 5.30am, and was barely awake when the phone rang.

'So how's it all going,' enthused Stephen Bumfrey from half way across the world. 'Yeah…uhm…not so bad thanks…I'm uhmm…just having a cup of tea!'

It was a terrible interview and I vowed never to be so badly prepared again. This time I had all the answers ready, ('15mph, 30 miles per day!'), and the presenter found the account of my breakdown on Scramblesby Hill hilarious, especially when I told her that I'd thought Lincolnshire was flat.

'So where are you off to next?' she asked.

'I'm going to be crossing the Humber Bridge in about an hour's time,' I replied. 'If anyone sees me please hoot!'

The presenter told me that the view from the Humber Bridge was spectacular, and that I'd really enjoy it. I hoped she was right. I'd been travelling mainly on quiet B-roads so far, and this would be the first time I'd be driving on a dual carriageway. Once I'd crossed the Humber, I would have about 20 miles to travel on the A63, which I was really dreading as I knew it would be full of impatient lorry drivers wanting to overtake.

After the interview, I made some last-minute phone calls (undertakers, life-insurance, that sort of thing!) and set off for the Humber Bridge. Finally completed in June 1981, the bridge is an engineering feat of real beauty, stretching 2,200 metres across the River Humber, at the time of completion the longest suspension bridge in the world. The south tower is sunk into the sand below the river, and a massive 44,000 miles of cable intertwine to reach across to the other side.

As I approached the start of the bridge, I was greeted by a big warning sign with 'Unusual Loads please stop and phone for permission to cross' written on it. I wasn't sure if that applied to me, but as the toll booths were on the other side, I figured it would be too late by the time I reached them for anyone to stop me. It was a fairly steep climb up to the bridge and we slowed down to about 5mph. Bluebell bumped over the joining sections of the bridge, which is designed to swing up to three metres in high winds, and I could feel it swaying as we reached the highest part.

After a while I noticed that Bluebell was the only vehicle in my lane, with the outside lane full of over-taking traffic. A group of walkers cheered me as I drove by, and I gave them a big wave. The view of the river was amazing, much wider than I'd expected, with big tankers floating beneath us. Crossing the Humber felt like a real milestone, as we left Norfolk well and truly behind and continued our journey north. When I finally reached the toll booth at the far end of the bridge, the lady that took my £1.50 had a huge grin on her face and said, 'I've never seen one of those before'. 'It's a milk float,' I proudly replied, and put my foot down on the accelerator before anyone could change their mind about letting us through!

It was raining by the time I reached the A63, and I was genuinely frightened as lorries thundered by, spraying water into our path. The road continued uphill for what seemed like forever, but Bluebell was handling it really well, doing a steady

15mph despite the gradient. I was willing the miles away, and shouted 'So long suckers' as Bluebell turned off onto the much more civilised B1230. I'd worked out my route with the help of a guy called Simon, aka Ambrose Blimfield, who'd booked me to perform that night at Naburn Station. Simon was also from the Milk Float Dimension, and used to go to festivals with a pink milk float that doubled up as a printing press.

I had to re-join the A63 for a while further along my route, but Simon had assured me the traffic was much thinner there, and it wasn't long before I was back onto country roads winding through rolling Yorkshire hills dotted with pretty farms. I was so happy that Bluebell had survived her first dual carriageway that I sang the rest of the way to Naburn! Ann, the owner of the hostel, wasn't around when I arrived, but I was made very welcome by Audrey, a lovely lady who was living in a caravan in the front garden with her two dogs.

After parking Bluebell and feeding some leads into the house to get her on charge, I went for a look round. The hostel had been converted from a station house, and had a great location right on the Trans Pennine Trail, with a cycle path following the river behind it. I asked Audrey if she was expecting many people for the gig that evening, and she said, 'If Simon's organising it, who knows!', which didn't sound too promising.

I sat around for the rest of the afternoon drinking tea and chatting to some of the backpackers who were coming and going. There was a communal feel to the place that reminded me of my days living in Glastonbury, although thankfully there were no King Arthurs or Guineveres wandering about, which had been a staple part of the Glastonbury scene. I finally heard back from Simon, who'd unexpectedly had to work for the evening, and said he wouldn't be able to make it along after all. It looked like the gig wasn't going to happen, but it had been such a tiring few days I felt it wouldn't do any harm to take the night off.

Ann turned up not long afterwards and was very apologetic that things hadn't been organised better. We spent the evening chatting, and she told me about how she'd had a radical lifestyle change after being a civil-servant for many years, and then bought Naburn Station with a friend. She now worked for a national cycle charity that encouraged people to get fit through cycling, and I admired her for opening her house up to other people in the way she had.

I went for a long walk along the river before it got dark, and retired back to Bluebell for an early night. I had a gig to get to the next day at a glamping site called The Hideaway at Baxby Manor, and a busy week ahead with more gigs to do in Barnard Castle and Hexham. And there was still the small matter of figuring out how I was going to cross the North Pennines, which would be the most challenging section of my tour so far.

FIVE

To Barnard Castle

I DIDN'T HAVE to be at the Hideaway at Baxby Manor until late afternoon, and had arranged with Simon to stop on the way to show him Bluebell, as he lived only a couple of miles outside York. It was a cold and wet day, and after I'd said my farewells to Ann and Audrey, Bluebell splashed her way through country lanes as far as the outskirts of York. Bleak House Farm lived up to its name, a dreary looking place with a few travellers living in caravans in a scruffy yard. I drove round a couple of times before stopping at a static caravan that I guessed must be Simon's. After knocking on the door, he eventually appeared looking as though he'd just woken up.

'Yours is much posher than mine,' said Simon, referring to Bluebell.

Simon had sold his milk float to buy parts for a pedal-powered music system that he was in the middle of building. His caravan was a mess of ash trays, empty beer cans, and half-finished inventions. It looked like there was a month's worth of washing-up in the sink, and I tentatively accepted his offer of a cup of tea. I was interested to know more about his inventions, though, which included a front-mounting bicycle trailer that he'd cycled with from York to Bristol. Simon gave me a demonstration of his pedal-powered music system, which had six bicycle seats mounted on a circular frame, with wires leading from the pedals into a generator. As Simon started pedalling, some lights lit up but I couldn't hear any music. 'There aren't any speakers attached yet,' explained Simon, who was still perfecting his invention!

Just before I left, one of Simon's friends turned up, carrying an armful of baby ducks. They were about the cutest things I've ever seen, with downy feathers and tiny beaks, and they followed Bluebell quacking away to the edge of the yard, where they stood watching as we disappeared from view.

The traffic around York ring road was fairly quiet due to it being Sunday, and after passing the castle we were soon out of the city onto a B-road, passing Sutton-on-the-Forest and Stillington, with traditional thick stone cottages nestling on village greens. I'd phoned Barney at the Hideaway to ask him directions the day before, and took a turning to avoid the Howardian Hills, which Barney had said were really steep. After stopping to ask directions at Husthwaite, I turned off just past the village onto a farm track that wove around a hall, leading to a beautiful wildflower meadow with all manner of tepees, camping pods and tents spread around.

Barney showed me my camping pod for the night, a lovely little wooden hobbit-type dwelling built with hexagonal walls, a sloping roof, and windows at ground level that looked out onto wildflowers. The rain had stopped, but there was still a bitter wind when I started setting up for the evening gig. A couple of local women from the village arrived while I was doing the soundcheck, and they set up camping stools in front of me.

'Can you hurry up please, I thought you were meant to start at 8 o'clock, and it's bloody freezing!' one of them said after a while.

Then the other one chipped in with, 'There are normally a lot more people here than this. Are you sure you want to play?'

I'd heard that Yorkshire people could be straight talking, but I didn't expect them to be this blunt!

'I've driven all the way from Norfolk in a milk float,' I replied, 'so I'm not going to give up now.'

'You came all the way in that just to play here?' heckler number one retorted.

'Well I didn't just come to play here, I'm on my way to the Edinburgh Fringe,' I explained.

I did my best to finish my soundcheck, by which time some of the campers had turned up, and looked on sympathetically as I dodged the hecklers' questions. It was the first chance I'd had to try out my new stage lights, which were running off the solar panels, and they worked really well giving my stage area a nice purple glow as night set in. Despite the cold, most of the campers came along to watch me play, and I stayed chatting to them for a while after the gig before returning to my little camping pod.

I was booked onto a campsite the next day at a place called Yafforth, about halfway to Barnard Castle, where I had a gig in two days. The wind had dropped, and it was lovely and sunny as Bluebell and I pulled away from the Hideaway for the next leg of our journey. Roadworks took us on a detour up a steep hill to the village of Carlton Husthwaite, which had a fantastic view of the Kilburn White Horse. Built by a local schoolmaster and volunteers in 1857, the horse stands proudly at 220 feet tall and 318 feet long, carved into the sandstone and filled with limestone chippings. I had no idea there were any hillside figures in the area, and the Kilburn White Horse is the most northerly in England.

After stopping briefly for some supplies at Thirsk, it was an easy ride to Northallerton, and then Yafforth a few miles further on. The camp site was fairly ordinary, except for an encampment of traditional gypsy wagons at the entrance, who'd pulled in off the main road for a free night's camping.

'Do you mind them being there?' I asked the camp site owner.

'Oh no, they're harmless,' he replied. 'They stop here every year on their way back from Appleby Fair.'

I was inquisitive to learn more about the gypsies, whose beautiful wagons were painted in bright colours with intricate designs around the edges of the frame, and I walked slowly past trying to pick up the courage to go and speak with them. In the end I decided that they'd probably prefer not to have their privacy invaded, which I could sympathise with. 'So what sort of speed do your horses do?' and, 'How many miles a day can you travel?' were probably not questions they wanted to be asked!

I managed to get lost in a boggy field behind the camp site instead, after trying to take a short-cut off the main path. What had been intended as a relaxing stroll ended up with me swearing and becoming increasingly frustrated, as my sandals sank further and further into the bog. Eventually reaching dry land again, I retreated back to Bluebell to cook supper and do some route planning. I had a long day ahead the next day, travelling 33 miles through hilly terrain to Barnard Castle, and then a radio interview at Teesdale Radio in the evening.

I was getting into a routine of waking about 7am, and after checking Bluebell's batteries had charged, would make breakfast whilst looking at my route for the day. I normally had a few tour-related jobs to catch up on, such as emailing venues and keeping my blog and social media pages updated, and after making a packed lunch for the journey, would get my map, satnav and travel bag together, ready to leave by about 10am. Somehow my little ritual gave me the confidence that I was going to make it to my next destination, although in truth I lived with the constant uncertainty that the next big hill could be my last.

I spent the morning addressing posters to send out for the Scottish part of my tour, and then set off towards Richmond. The hills were becoming gradually bigger, and I felt a twinge of anticipation as the Pennines came into view in the distance, which I'd be crossing in a few days. The hill into Richmond was much steeper than I'd expected, and I had a queue of cars behind me on the long ascent into town. After passing a castle in the town centre, the satnav guided me unexpectedly up an even steeper hill, and I could smell burning coming from Bluebell's motor. Spotting a housing estate on my right, I pulled in to let her cool down for a while, and had a look at my map.

An elderly man who'd been doing some gardening was looking at me inquisitively, and I went over to ask him directions. He stared at the map for a while and then said, 'Hang on I'll go and get my glasses.' Although I'd come a different route than I'd planned, he said it was mostly downhill the way I was going, which suited me just fine. I sat in the cab for a while eating a sandwich to give Bluebell longer to cool down, and a man delivering newspapers stopped to tell me he'd read about my tour, and said he was going to come along and watch me play at Barnard Castle the following night. Fame at last!

Eventually I plucked up the courage to drive up the remainder of the hill, and breathed a sigh of relief as we came to the top. The countryside past Richmond was spectacular, with wide rivers, ravines, and sprawling farms on high hills with no sight of houses for miles. After climbing another couple of hills, I stopped by a wood to let Bluebell cool down again, and had a nap in the back, dozing off to the tranquil sounds of my surroundings. We still had a long way to go, and afterwards continued down a steep hill towards a village called Ravensworth which led to the A66.

We soon had a massive queue behind us, but thankfully I'd worked out a plan B to get us the rest of the way to Barnard Castle, and turned off almost immediately onto more country lanes. The battery meter had been flashing red for several miles, but Bluebell was running as strong as ever by the time we came into Barnard Castle. I'd spent a night there a few years previously on my way back from a holiday in Scotland, but hadn't had a chance to explore it properly. The town was much prettier than I'd remembered, built in a steep valley with narrow streets climbing from its centre, and a beautiful castle overlooking the river.

My campsite was a few miles out of town, and I wanted to check-in before returning to do my interview at the Radio Teesdale studio that evening. It was further than I'd thought, but eventually we turned off onto a farm track with a steep downhill into the site. I managed to get a couple of hours charge into Bluebell and cook some supper before heading back into town for my radio interview. Just as we got to the bottom of the steep hill leading out of the campsite, a horse-rider turned out from a field, and we had to slow down behind her. She kept trying to wave me past, but didn't realise I was already going as fast as I could! The only way to get Bluebell up steep hills was with a good run-up, so I reversed back down the hill to have another go. The horse-rider had stopped at the top of the hill and was watching me with a strange expression as I sped past her, punching the air and shouting, 'good girl Bluebell!'

When I arrived at the Radio Teesdale studio Liz Franklin, the presenter, was standing at the door waving and grinning at me. We just had time to reel a couple of leads into the building to get some more charge in Bluebell, before heading off to the studio. A duo called Karin and Rosie were also on the show, and we had a quick tuning session of our guitars before going live on-air. Liz was a fantastic lady, with an infectious and bubbly personality, a true supporter of independent musicians. We chatted about my tour, and I played four songs over the next couple of hours, taking it in turns with Karin and Rosie, who were also promoting a new album. For some strange reason, there was a life-size cardboard cut-out of a cow in the studio, which we carried outside for some photos next to Bluebell afterwards. Liz said she'd be along the next night to watch me play at the Witham Arts Centre, where I was also running a songwriting workshop for a group of school children.

It was raining when I woke the next day, and I spent the morning doing some preparation for the workshop I was running in the afternoon, and phoned my dad to see how he was. He had an operation scheduled in a week's time, but there were problems due to him having a heart condition which might prevent him being able to have the anaesthetic. I was really worried for him, and wished I could have been there to provide some moral support, but he told me how proud he was of what I was doing and that I must carry on.

When I got into town the rain had stopped, and I took the opportunity to set my music gear up in the venue before the children arrived for the workshop. They were a mixed age group from 10 to 16, and I was immediately impressed by how accepting and encouraging of one another they were. We went for a walk to the castle to get some inspiration for our writing, and found some stone statues in a circle that were perfect for triggering the imagination. After wandering around the grounds and along the river, we returned to the Witham and did some song-lyric writing, using the notes everyone had taken on the walk. It amazed me how different everyone's writing was, and by the time we finished there were some really interesting song ideas taking shape.

The workshop had only just finished when a journalist from BBC Radio Tees turned up to do an interview. Sheltering round the back of Bluebell from the wind, the journalist asked me some questions, and then suggested doing a video of me playing a song. I had to fetch all my music gear out from the venue, and was just putting it back afterwards when the journalist said, 'I'm really sorry but could we do it again. I put my thumb across the picture by mistake.' Ever the true professional, I gritted my teeth and played the song again!

Not long afterwards my support act for the night turned up, a singer-songwriter from Huddersfield called Sam H. It was the first time we'd met, although Sam and I had been communicating for a while by email, and it was nice to have a chance to find out more about each other. Sam worked as a full-time musician, playing solo as well as in a band with his friend Jade, who'd given him a lift to the gig. A retired couple called Margaret and Angus who were keen supporters of the Witham had kindly offered to put us all up for the night, and they came over to say hello before the show started.

Sam performed a great set, and had the audience nicely warmed up by the time I took to the stage. Liz Franklin was in the audience beaming big smiles as I played, and I really enjoyed performing the songs from my album, sensing that the audience were appreciating the show. My bubble was burst slightly when a man came up to me afterwards and said, 'That was absolutely brilliant, but I couldn't understand a bloody word of it.' He'd apparently been harassing some of the staff, who'd called the police as he was obviously drunk, and had parked his car outside the venue.

The man eventually disappeared, and I got packed up so that I could go back to Angus and Margaret's house. Bluebell would be safely locked behind the gates of the Witham for the night, and after saying goodbye to Liz Franklin, I jumped in Jade's Mini and we headed off for a pit-stop in town for some pizza. Angus was waiting up for us when we got back, and we sat round his big kitchen table chatting for a while. It was a luxury to have a decent bed for the night, and it wasn't long before I was fast asleep.

Angus and Margaret's grand-daughters called in on their way to school the next morning to cook us all breakfast, and afterwards Angus said that he'd take us for a walk around town. Angus was a fountain of knowledge about Barnard Castle, which had been an important mill town, and as an ex-architect he knew the history of all the old buildings. When we got back to Angus and Margaret's house, Sam and Jade said their goodbyes as they had to get back to Huddersfield, and I was glad that I'd be seeing them later in the summer when they'd be coming to perform in Edinburgh for three days.

Before I left, I went over my route to Hexham with Angus and Margaret, as I was worried that the road I'd planned to travel on might be too hilly for Bluebell. We worked out an alternative route via Bishop Auckland avoiding a steep section of the A68, that would take me to a place called Fir Tree, where I was booked into a camp site for the night. I'd still be faced with the biggest hills of my tour the following day, further up the A68 at a place called Castleside, but my only other option was to go directly across the top of the North Pennines, which I'd thought would be too hilly, and would take me an extra day to reach Hexham.

After thanking Angus and Margaret for their kindness I walked back into town and fetched Bluebell. The road to

Bishop Auckland was mainly downhill, passing a lovely old castle called Raby on the way. The route I'd worked out took me through Bishop Auckland onto a flat B-road that went through a village called Toronto, which I suspected had been shrunk and moved from Canada due to travelling in the Milk Float Dimension!

The Greenhead Campsite at Fir Tree doubled up as an old-fashioned country hotel, run by an ex milkman with ruddy cheeks and a booming voice. It was a beautiful hotel with an ancient grandfather clock chiming away in the corner, and filled with antique furniture. The owner told me how the place had once been a dairy, with a fleet of milk floats in the yard. I was keen to know which route he thought I should take the next day.

'I should go across the Pennines if I were you,' he said. 'Straight to Alston and then down to Hexham from there. There's no really big hills that way,' he assured me.

As he'd been a milkman for 30 years, I felt I should take his advice, and worked out that if I stopped halfway along the Pennines, I wouldn't have far to go the day after to get me to my gig in Hexham. There was nobody else on the campsite at Fir Trees, and I had a restful day cooking myself a curry in the evening, and going for a walk up a huge hill with views across to the Pennines. As I gazed across the Northumberland hills I pondered my journey so far. I'd now travelled over 350 miles in two weeks, and all being well would be across the Scottish border in a week. Life in the Milk Float Dimension was good, and with views like this what could possibly go wrong?

SIX

Never Trust a Milkman!

It was bitterly cold when I set off for Hagg's Bank Bunkhouse, the campsite at the top of the North Pennines that I'd booked for the night. From Fir Tree, I was almost immediately onto the A689, a spectacular road that cuts directly across the Pennines to Penrith. I passed miles of thick lichen-covered stone walls, bordering buttercup fields full of grazing cows, beyond that the moors spreading off into the distance towards Northumberland. The road was hilly, but nothing too steep for Bluebell to handle, and we made good progress through the towns of Wolsingham and Stanhope.

After passing a couple of mining museums, we came into a deep and lonely looking valley with just a single farmhouse surrounded by felled trees. I didn't like the look of the hill on the far side, which was incredibly steep at the top, and I pulled in to let Bluebell cool down before we tackled it. I was becoming used to my middle of nowhere snoozes, and with both Bluebell and myself suitably rested, I climbed back in the cab, turned the ignition and drove towards the hill. We slowed to about 5mph by the time we passed the farmhouse halfway up, and managed about another 300 yards before the motor finally ground to a halt. We were now on the steepest part of the hill, and I had to jam the brake on to stop Bluebell slipping backwards. I realised there was no way she'd be able to get up the last section, even if I gave the motor more time to cool down.

There was no signal on my phone, so I ran back down to the farmhouse to see if somebody could help. I was greeted at the locked gates by a sign that said 'Banks Foot – You Are Being Watched!' Somewhere out of view a vicious sounding dog was barking, and I stood calling 'hello' for a while, until eventually a man came out and said, 'Where's the dog?'.

'I don't know,' I replied, 'I'm travelling in a milk float and I've got stuck near the top of the hill. Would there be any chance of towing me the rest of the way up?'

'I'll have to go and ask my wife,' he said, and left me standing in the freezing cold on the other side of the gate.

It was a very strange place, with a few grubby clothes drying on the washing line, and not a sign of any flowers in the rubble strewn garden. After a while the man came back and said, 'My wife says we can't tow you because we're not covered on the insurance.'

'Could you phone the camp site, and see if they could tow me?' I asked, and gave him the number.

The man left me standing at the gates for another ten minutes, until he came back and said that he'd talked to a lady called Kathy at Hagg's Bank Bunkhouse, and that she'd be along with a neighbour as soon as she could. It wasn't long before Kathy turned up with Pete in a Land Rover, both waving and smiling as they approached. Pete soon had a rope tied onto the front of Bluebell ready to tow her up the remaining part of the hill.

'I'll take you to the top,' he said, 'and then you can freewheel downhill to the campsite'.

'And I'll put the kettle on ready for you arriving,' said Kathy.

Bluebell jerked forwards as she took the strain of the rope, and we were soon at the top of the hill with an amazing view over the Pennines. Pete unhooked the rope, and Bluebell freewheeled the rest of the way down the hill. As promised, Kathy had the kettle on, and I sat in her mobile home for a while getting warm by the fire. We had quite a lot in common as she'd grown up in Norwich, but now lived in Penrith, spending part of the week staying at the campsite where she was the manager.

Kathy told me that she had to get ready for a group of moth enthusiasts who were camping for the night, but that I could pop back later for another cup of tea and to use the computer. I was parked next to an old bus that had been converted into a campervan by its owner, Mike, a lovely guy who'd been living in Scotland but was returning to Durham, where he'd spent his childhood. When I told Mike the route I was taking the next day to Hexham, he said he was really worried that it would be too hilly for Bluebell. After cooking supper, I went back to Kathy's mobile home for a cup of tea, and when I told her what Mike had said she kindly offered to drive me on the route I was planning, so that I could see what the hills were like before tackling them.

We were soon on a narrow road leading over the moors

that was incredibly beautiful, but also impossibly steep. I could see for miles and miles, probably as far as the border with Scotland, but there was no signal on my phone, no houses in sight, and I realised that I'd be well and truly stranded if things went wrong. I still had the option of going via Alston, which was the way the milkman had suggested, but it would mean climbing a long and steep hill called the Whitfield Bends before getting to Hexham. When I told Kathy about the advice I'd been given to come this way, she said, 'Well, you know what they say…never trust a milkman!'

Kathy drove me up the Whitfield Bends, and although the hill was steep and long, it didn't seem as extreme as my alternate route across the moors. The only part that worried me was a sharp U-bend about half way up that I'd have to corner on the wrong side of the road if I wanted to keep enough momentum to reach the top of the hill. When we got back to the campsite the moth enthusiasts had turned up with some huge white sheets that they'd fixed in the trees near the camping area, with lights shining on them to attract the moths. They were planning an all-night vigil which I politely declined joining in with, as I had a long day ahead. It would be a minor miracle if I made it over the top of the Pennines the next day, and I was worried that if I did break down it would mean missing my gig in the evening.

I was on the road early the next day and said thank you to Kathy, waving goodbye to her and Mike as I drove Bluebell towards the Whitfield Bends. We passed through the lovely market town of Alston, the highest in England, with cobbled streets and a beautiful old church at its centre with a stone spire. After that we climbed for about five miles across the moors until we reached the Northumberland border sign, and I stopped to take a photo of Bluebell next to it, proud that we'd made it all this way from Norfolk. I wanted to make sure that Bluebell's motor was cool enough before climbing the Whitfield Bends, and stopped again another five miles along the road for a cup of tea. I was just finishing it off when a couple of elderly ladies came up to me who'd parked in the lay-by.

'You look very contented there,' one of them said.

I told them about my adventure, and after a while one of them produced a leaflet and said, 'Would you mind if I gave you one of these?'

I have to say I've been approached by a few Jehovah's Witnesses before, but never whilst sitting in a milk float in the middle of the Northumberland Moors! Credit where it's due, at least they were committed to their beliefs. I told them that religion wasn't really for me, but asked if they would say a little prayer to help me get up the Whitfield Bends. With God on my side I set off up the hill, which was much longer and steeper in the Milk Float Dimension than it had seemed in Kathy's car the day before. As we approached the U-bend, I pulled onto the other side of the road as the motor slowed, shouting my mantra, 'Come on Bluebell, you can do it!'

At one point we almost stalled, but Bluebell just managed to keep going, and made it over the steepest part. There were still another couple of miles to climb, but it was all gradual, and as we came to the top of the hill I felt a surge of elation that we'd conquered the North Pennines together. It was downhill from there all the way to the A69, which we followed for another few miles until we turned off towards Hexham. Eventually we reached the town centre and parked outside the Forum Cinema, where I was running a songwriting workshop that afternoon and playing an evening gig.

Despite the event having gained a fair amount of local press coverage, there was nobody there by the time the workshop was due to start, and it looked like it was going to be a 'no-show'. All was not lost, however, when Joan and Jim, an elderly retired couple turned up and asked if they were in the right place. We were soon deep in discussion about song writing, and we decided to go for a walk around town to get some ideas for songs. I was impressed by Joan and Jim's willingness to give new things a go, and it wasn't long before I had them both hugging trees in a park and closing their eyes by the river to get them tuned into their senses.

I had a young local singer-songwriter called Sam Robinson doing a support slot, who arrived later with his family and friends, and he played some lovely original songs before I did my first set of the evening. During the interval, a lady called Marianne turned up who'd offered to let me park Bluebell outside her house for the night. She said she had to go and pick her children up from a party, but explained where I needed to go and said that she'd see me later.

It was almost midnight by the time I arrived at Marianne's, and her children helped me tape my cables to the pavement in torchlight so that I could get Bluebell on charge. Afterwards they invited me in for a hot chocolate, and Marianne's daughter, who was learning to play guitar, sang a beautiful song that she'd written. Marianne was getting up again in a few hours with the children for a game of dawn golf to celebrate the summer solstice, and said that she'd see me when they got back. It was a strange feeling falling asleep on the streets of Hexham, and every now and then a group of revellers would walk past on their way home from the pub, making some comment or other about Bluebell (although thankfully nobody urinated on her – at least not that I know of!).

I slept in late the next morning, and sat drinking cups of tea in the back of Bluebell until Marianne returned. After breakfast, Bluebell and I got on the road to Hadrian's Wall. I was due to be running a songwriting workshop and doing a gig at a Northumberland National Park centre called Once Brewed, and was really looking forward to it. Ever since I'd had the idea of touring to Scotland, for some reason I'd had an image in my mind of performing along Hadrian's Wall on the summer solstice. After contacting several venues, I eventually discovered Once Brewed, who were perfectly located just half a mile from the Wall, and were really keen on me playing there.

Hexham is only about 15 miles away from Once Brewed, and I was expecting a fairly easy journey. How wrong I was! After passing the village of Wall, we turned onto the B6318, which follows Hadrian's Wall as it climbs up and down the steep Northumberland hills. Bluebell was really struggling, and after grinding to a halt on one hill, we were only just able to crawl into a car park half a mile further along. I phoned Karen at Once Brewed to explain that I was having problems, and she said I'd have to be really careful as the road got hillier ahead, and there were hidden dips that would be dangerous if I got stuck again.

Reluctantly I phoned the AA, who said a recovery vehicle would be there as soon as possible. It was raining and freezing cold, and I sat dejectedly in Bluebell watching the soaking wet walkers returning to the car park from the hills. Eventually the AA man turned up and told me that he couldn't do any repairs to the milk float as it was an electric vehicle, but said he would tow me to Once Brewed, which was about five miles away. He hitched a solid tow bar onto Bluebell, and we were soon being pulled up and down some massive hills. After a couple of miles I could smell burning coming from the motor, and by the time we reached Once Brewed and un-hitched Bluebell she wouldn't start at all. I got the AA man to reverse us into position on the car park, where Karen had said I could stay the night, and realised that I'd have to worry about Bluebell in the morning, as I'd already missed the workshop and had my gig to prepare for that night.

Karen and all the staff at Once Brewed were really friendly, supplying me with hot drinks and sandwiches as I set up for the gig. I was about to begin when a mass of cars turned up in the car park. Unfortunately they weren't for me, but had come to rescue a walker who'd gone missing in the hills. We decided to wait a while before starting the gig, and we all stood at the window watching the drama unfold before us. There was a lot of talking into walkie-talkies going on, with more and more rescue vehicles and police cars arriving, but there didn't seem to be a lot of action taking place. Eventually a bedraggled walker turned up looking very sorry for himself, accompanied by a couple of the mountain rescue team. Apparently the man had taken a wrong turning and lost the rest of his group, who'd raised the alarm.

Every cloud has a silver lining, and I now had a ready-made audience as everyone came into Once Brewed to get warm afterwards. I had the most fantastic view of Hadrian's Wall out of the window, and it turned out to be one of my best gigs so far. At the end of the night Karen said I could leave my music gear set up where it was and come back for it in the morning. I still didn't know whether any real damage had been done to Bluebell's motor, and just hoped that by the next day she'd have had time to cool down, and would start as normal.

There were times on my tour when the way things worked out made me think that somebody or something was looking over me when I needed help the most. I'd been given one phone number by John from CBL to ring if I had mechanical problems, and it just so happened that Gary from EVS Electrical was only an hour away from Once Brewed. There was still no sign of life in Bluebell when I tried the ignition the next morning, so I gave Gary a ring and he said he'd be there as soon as he could. Karen in Once Brewed was ever helpful, telling me I could use their toilets to wash in, and offering me an endless supply of tea and cakes.

It wasn't long before Gary turned up with his apprentice Tony, and were submerged beneath the floorboards of Bluebell running tests on the motor and controller. I didn't want to get in their way, so I went back into Once Brewed to catch up on some emails, popping back out every now and then to check on their progress. Each time I came out there seemed to be more wires undone, and Gary would sigh and say, 'It's not looking good I'm afraid'. He explained how towing the vehicle at the speed we did had probably burnt the motor out, and there was a chance that the controller had also been damaged as a result. The only way to find out for sure would be to take the motor out, and for a specialist to inspect it. A new motor would cost £5,000, which I couldn't have afforded, but he said there was a chance that it could be re-built for about £1,000.

To remove the motor would mean first taking Bluebell to a garage so that Gary could get underneath the chassis, and Karen found me the number of a local recovery operator who was based at a garage a couple of miles away at Henshaw. Luckily, there was a Youth Hostel next to Once Brewed that I managed to book into for the night, and I hurriedly packed some things into my suitcase as we waited for the recovery lorry to arrive. Gary was planning to take the motor to his contact in Durham the next day, and said he'd be in touch as soon as he knew whether it could be repaired. I watched in dismay as Bluebell was loaded onto the recovery truck, wondering if this was the end of the tour. Just as the lorry was pulling away, a strange-looking guy on a moped turned up with a saxophone on his back.

'Are you Paul?', he asked.

'Yes,' I replied.

'I'm Stefan,' he continued. 'I'm from Norfolk. I read about your tour and have been trying to catch you up.'

This was all I needed. My home and tour bus had just been taken away, and now I had a stalker to contend with who'd followed me all the way from Norfolk on a moped!

'Are you staying at the hostel tonight?' enquired Stefan.

'Looks like it,' I reluctantly replied.

'Great so am I,' said Stefan.

I made my excuses and went over to speak to Gary, who was packing all his tools into his van. He'd spent most of the day working on Bluebell and only charged me £50 for his time, which was incredibly kind, as it probably should have been three or four times that amount. I think Gary was quite taken by the idea of my journey, and he seemed to understand that I didn't have a great deal of spare cash.

After he'd gone, I collected my suitcase and went to check in at the hostel. I was hoping that Stefan would be in a different dorm room, but worse luck when I opened the door, there he was sitting on a bed with nobody else in the room. Stefan's clothes were filthy, and he had all his possessions spread out on the floor drying out. I was emotionally exhausted and too tired to make polite conversation, and fell asleep in my bunk. When I woke up an hour later there was no sign of Stefan, and I took the opportunity to phone my dad to tell him about the breakdown.

'I knew something like this would happen,' he said. 'I've put some money aside for you if you need it.'

I was touched that my dad was thinking about me when he had so many worries of his own to contend with. He told me to keep my spirits up and that things would seem brighter the next day. I went down to the cafe to try and cheer myself up with a hot meal, but ended up watching the groups of walkers, feeling even more alone as they laughed and talked about their day. It felt so strange to be separated from Bluebell, and to not have my small creature comforts around me anymore. I realised how attached I'd become to my four-wheeled companion, and I worried about her spending the night on her own in the garage.

After I'd finished eating I went for a walk, and the fresh-air and views across the Northumberland hills soon helped to put things back into perspective. I'd been reading about the history of Hadrian's Wall in the Once Brewed Centre, which had some display boards up with information about its construction. Work started on the wall in 122 AD, under the orders of the emperor Hadrian. Stretching 72 miles from the banks of the Tyne in the east to the Salway Firth in the west, it took six years to complete, and rose up to 20 feet high. I was amazed by how much of the Wall was still intact, which must have looked incredible when it was first completed, as it was also thought to have been whitewashed.

I followed a path along the Wall through a valley with a huge sycamore tree at the bottom, and walked up the other side where I was greeted by a spectacular view over a lake, with shafts of light pouring down onto the hills behind. It was almost dark by the time I got back to the Youth Hostel, and Stefan was sitting in the foyer waiting for me. He'd changed clothes, and was now wearing a 1920s style zoot-suit with penguin shoes and a purple beret. I felt suddenly guilty that I hadn't really given Stefan a chance, even if he did seem slightly eccentric. After all, I was travelling the country in a milk float and could hardly be described as normal myself!

Stefan started telling me about his life as a musician, and how he'd also done unusual tours by horse and cart, and with a band on mopeds. We chatted for about an hour, and arranged to play some music together the next day as it didn't look like I'd be going anywhere for a while. As I lay in bed I reflected on the tour so far, wondering what the future would bring. If the tour was over, it would still have been an incredible adventure. Bluebell and I had crossed the Humber Bridge and North Pennines, almost reaching the Scottish border, when many people had predicted that I wouldn't get further than Norfolk. I'd run a songwriting workshop from the top of a wind turbine, and played gigs in some amazing locations. But as I thought of Bluebell alone in a garage, I knew that somehow I must find a way of getting her back on the road again. After all, we were expected in Scotland, and I wasn't going to let a 2,000 year-old wall get in the way!

SEVEN

Border Crossing

I PHONED GARY at EVS the next morning to see how things were going, and he said he wouldn't know until the next day if the repair could be done on the motor. I booked into the hostel for another night, and grabbed my guitar before they closed for the day. Stefan was outside playing his saxophone, and I suggested we go for a walk to Hadrian's Wall. While we were walking up there, Stefan suddenly said out of the blue, 'So what makes you think just because you write your own music people want to listen to it?' I was slightly taken aback, and sensed that for some reason Stefan was trying to provoke me. When I didn't react, he started ranting about how hard his life was as a jobbing musician, and his personality seemed to have completely changed from the previous night.

I tried to put the conversation aside, and when we reached Hadrian's Wall suggested we have a jam. Stefan said he wanted to teach me a jazz song, but when I started playing he grabbed my guitar off me, saying, 'Not like that. This is how you do it'. I was in no mood for being bullied, and after taking my guitar back, I silently packed it away, and walked off leaving Stefan playing his saxophone alone on the Wall. When I got back to

Once Brewed, I told Karen what had happened and she said if I wanted to avoid Stefan I could sit in their garden until the hostel opened again. Stefan had packed his panniers on the moped before we went for our walk, and had said he was planning to leave later that day. Eventually I heard the sound of his moped starting up and disappearing into the distance, and thankfully that was the last I saw or heard from Stefan.

I still needed to figure out how I was going to get to my next gig in Scotland, which was in a place called Moffat. My carefully planned route with Bluebell was now well and truly behind schedule, but I was determined not to cancel any shows unless I really had to. After phoning around a few car-hire companies, I found one that could deliver a car to the hostel, and then take me back to the garage to collect Bluebell when the hire was over. I needed to move on the next day as Once Brewed was fully booked, and had found another hostel to stay at in Bellingham, on the edge of Kielder Forest Park.

That evening I went to the local pub for a bite to eat, and made some phone calls to let the next few venues know that there was a problem with Bluebell. I was due to be doing a house concert in Moffat, just over the Scottish border, for a guy called John Weatherby who was a professional sound engineer. I was worried that John might not want me to come now that I didn't have Bluebell, but when I spoke to him, he just said, 'Ach, come for as long as you need to. It's not a problem'.

I had another couple of gigs lined up on the way to Ardrossan, where I was due to be catching a ferry to Campbeltown on the Mull of Kintyre. Every day that Bluebell was off the road meant another day of travelling lost, and the only way I could see to make up time would be to hire a transporter lorry, which would be really costly. There was still no guarantee that the motor could be fixed, and the whole tour might be off by the next day anyway, but I tried to stay positive. I had phone calls from all my family that night wishing me well, and I felt so glad of their support, especially after the argument I'd had with Stefan earlier in the day. I now had the dormitory all to myself, and grateful for small mercies I went to bed early with a book, hopeful that the next day would bring better news.

Gary phoned me at 10 o'clock the next morning to let me know that his contact had looked at the motor, and said it could be repaired. It was a complicated job involving re-coiling the inside, replacing the armature and outer varnish, and then baking the motor for at least 24 hours. I had no idea that motors could be baked, but I'd learnt to come to expect anything in the Milk Float Dimension! It was fantastic news, although Gary did say that he wouldn't know until the motor was fitted whether I'd need a new controller, which would mean more costs and time out from the tour, as the controller would take a couple of days to be ordered and fitted.

I felt a huge surge of relief now that the tour was back on, and went to let Karen know. She'd been such a good friend over the last few days, never making me feel as if I was in the way, and I thanked her for all her kindness, and told her I'd keep in touch. It wasn't long before the hire-car arrived, a shiny black hatchback that would be just the right size for fitting my music gear in. I stopped at Henshaw Garage to collect some items from Bluebell, and felt sad seeing her loaded at a steep angle on the lorry, looking sorry for herself.

It was a very strange feeling driving a car again after being in the Milk Float Dimension for the last three weeks, and I didn't feel safe driving at more than 50mph. It was only 30 miles to Bellingham, and I couldn't get my head round the fact that I'd got there in half an hour instead of half a day! I had a nice hostel to stay in for the night, a barn conversion with a plush kitchen and a wood-burning stove in the communal lounge. The place was empty when I arrived, so I bagged the best bed in the dorm, next to a flue which rose up from the wood-burner in the room below. Despite being mid-summer, it was still cold, and I had to get under the bed covers to keep warm for my afternoon siesta.

After cooking a salmon supper, I drove to the top of a valley to phone my dad as I couldn't get a signal in the hostel. I wished him all the best for his operation, which was the next day, and made my mind up that if needed I'd drive back to Norfolk in the hire car, even if it meant having to miss more dates on the tour. When I got back to the hostel, a few people were sitting in the lounge and I struck up a conversation with a guy called Steve, who'd retired to Spain but had returned to England for a few weeks to walk the Pennine Way. It sounded like a tough walk, but Steve seemed to be coping with it admirably despite some inevitable aches and pains.

I told Steve about the milk float tour which he thought was fantastic, and he asked if I'd mind playing a couple of songs for everyone. I fetched my guitar and played a song from my first album called 'The Morning Light', which I thought would appeal to Steve as it's about waking up to a new day and appreciating the beauty of nature. He absolutely loved it and said how talented he thought I was, which was just what I needed to hear after the conversation I'd had with Stefan the day before.

The drive through Kielder Forest Park to the Scottish border the next day was incredible. I followed a narrow road through isolated villages, and then along the length of Kielder Water to the village of Kielder, which has a castle and a steep walk up to a disused viaduct with far-reaching views across the park. Kielder Water is entirely manmade, the largest reservoir in the UK, holding 200 billion litres of water, and the pine trees that surround it form the largest manmade forest in Europe, spreading for 250 square miles. Commissioned by the British government in the 1920s, the trees were planted by the Forestry Commission as part of a national policy to increase timber reserves, and remain state owned to this day.

As I approached the Scottish border, I felt disappointed that I wasn't crossing it in Bluebell, but it was probably for the best as she wouldn't have coped with the mountainous terrain. The scenery became gradually wilder, passing traditional Scottish stone cottages and bridges that crossed fast-flowing rocky rivers. Before arriving in Moffat, I phoned my brother to see how things were with my dad. It wasn't good news. They'd taken him in for the operation, but his blood pressure had been too low, so they'd had to cancel and weren't sure if they'd be able to do the operation at all. It would mean another appointment with a consultant, and meanwhile the time-bomb of cancer was ticking. It must have been awful for my dad having to cope with so much uncertainty, and I realised that my own problems were small compared to his.

John and his partner Mairi couldn't have been more welcoming when I arrived in Moffat. After telling John that I needed to find a way of transporting Bluebell to make up for lost time, he offered to try and get hold of a trailer for me. I was touched by his kindness, and when I offered to pay him, he just said, 'Don't be daft, we'll see what we can sort out'. He showed me his studio, which had microphones set up everywhere and a control room with a window looking out onto the area where I'd be performing. I was instantly at home, and looking forward to playing for John's friends, who'd be along in a couple of hours.

Mairi cooked us a lovely meal of home baked macaroni cheese with garlic bread, new potatoes, and strawberries with ice cream and Pavlova for dessert. Not long after, the guests started arriving and we chatted for a while in John's livingroom before heading through to the studio. I'd promised John that I'd tell some stories from the tour, and I soon had everyone in stitches as I recounted my various breakdowns. The worrying part was how much they laughed when I said I'd be carrying on to the Outer Hebrides, and somebody quipped, 'They've got one or two hills up there as well you know.'

I stayed up chatting to John and Mairi for a while after the gig, and just before I went to bed John produced a big jar with money in it. Everyone had given really generously, but when I offered John some of the proceeds, he wouldn't accept anything. John said I could stay for the next few days until I knew what was happening with Bluebell, and that he'd make some enquiries the next day into hiring a trailer. I was exhausted by the time I got to bed, but thankful to have found such a safe haven in my time of need.

John spent the next morning phoning round trailer-hire companies, but wasn't able to find a trailer that could take the weight of Bluebell. He said that he'd call in to see a guy called Willy at the local garage, who had a recovery lorry and might be able to help. We were due to be going to Crawford John, a small village about 20 miles away, where John was doing the sound that night for a gig. After an early lunch we stopped at John's lock-up to load some music equipment into his van. I'd never seen a space crammed full of so much music equipment in all my life, with speakers piled up to the ceiling, shelves full of microphones, and cables hanging from every orifice. I asked John how he'd got into the music business, and he told me he'd started out helping another sound engineer, and eventually taken over the business when the engineer retired. Like me, he obviously had a reluctance to throw things away due to 'just in case I might need it again one day syndrome'.

Willy from the local garage was a slightly forbidding character, with a ferocious-looking Alsatian at his side. But like his dog, Willy's bark proved to be worse than his non-existent bite, and he said he'd do his best to help. John and I set off for Crawford John, a pretty village with a small churchyard, a few houses, and lovely stone walls surrounding the farmland that spread from its outskirts. We had plenty of time to set up for the evening gig, which was being held in the village hall. A well-known Celtic band was playing, who were due to be performing at Glastonbury, and I was looking forward to hearing them.

John said there wasn't very much I could do to help, so I went for a walk to idle away some time before the gig. I followed a road up a steep hill, passing little forest tracks that meandered around streams. Every time I stopped to admire the view I was surrounded by a cloud of midges, and eventually I got fed up with it, walking back to the village to get something to eat from the pub. An extremely pretty French waitress came over to my table, and as she took the menu, our eyes locked and everything seemed to go into slow motion. I smiled and said thank you, and when she walked past a while later and our eyes met again, I wondered if I should ask her if she was going to the gig once she'd finished work. After I'd eaten my meal, I sat hoping she might come back out again, but there was still no sign of her when I finally left.

I walked slowly back to the village hall fantasizing about us meeting again later that night, but ended up sitting next to an 80-year-old man called Hamish for the evening! Hamish lived in a nearby village, and had a passion for Celtic music. He was soon telling me the history of the bagpipes, as well as his own family history, that reached as far as Nova Scotia. The band was fantastic, and sang all their songs in Gaelic. There was a real sense of Scottish pride on display in the hall, with several men dressed in kilts, and the audience got up from their seats to clap along and dance to the traditional tunes. I loved the combination of instruments, with acoustic guitar, piano accordion, bagpipes, and two fiddles playing harmony parts. As the night drew to a close, there was still no sign of the French waitress, and after saying goodbye to Hamish it was time to go.

I slept in late the following morning, and when John eventually surfaced we went into Moffat to have a look round a classic car-rally that was taking place on the local playing-fields. It turned out that John was a bit of an enthusiast, and he hadn't told me that he had a classic MG parked in his garage that he was planning on taking me for a spin in later. After looking at cars for a while we went for a wander round Moffat, which has the only high street in Britain with a two-way street on either side of the road. Once a popular spa town, Moffat was also a centre of the wool trade and has a statue of a ram in between the two main streets. Hamish had asked me the night before if I'd noticed anything unusual about the ram, and it took me a while to figure out that it didn't have any ears!

John gave me a guided tour of the area when we set off in his MG later that afternoon. A particularly gruesome piece of local history John told me about was of a notorious murder case from the 1930s, committed by an Indian doctor called Buck Roxton. The possessive doctor had married an English socialite, and murdered her in a fit of jealousy, also killing their maid who it's thought had witnessed the crime. Roxton dismembered the bodies, travelling all the way from Lancaster with them in the boot of his car, before disposing of the pieces in a stream two miles outside of Moffat. He was eventually caught after police discovered the bodies had been wrapped in a specialist newspaper. The investigating officer tracked down all the subscribers, and put two and two together after discovering that Roxton had been stopped by a policeman on his way home, after knocking a cyclist off his bike in the Lake District. Pioneering forensic evidence proved the rest, and the doctor was hanged for his crime.

John's gory tale reminded me of an incident when I was on tour in Alaska a few years previously. I was hitch-hiking to a gig in the south of Alaska at a place called Homer, when a guy pulled over, and as he put my music gear in the boot of the car, said jokingly, 'Plenty of room in here for dead bodies!' Of course, I was fairly sure it was a joke, but when he said further along the road, 'I've been meaning to do a hike up this mountain for a while, would you mind if we stopped to do it?', I started to get worried.

'Yes, sure' I replied, but as we climbed higher into the mountains, I was imagining those dead bodies in the trunk of his car, and wondering if I was about to be pushed off the edge of a precipice! Luckily for me it turned out that Pat was in fact a really nice family guy, and he told me about his life growing up on Kodiak Island, one of the remotest islands in Alaska. I became good friends with Pat and his family, who invited me to a BBQ at their house the following day, and came along to a few of my gigs.

I phoned Gary the next day to see how things were going with Bluebell's motor, and he said he would be at Henshaw garage to fit it the following day. If all went well, I could return the hire car, and Willy would come and pick Bluebell up in the evening, taking us 30 or 40 miles past Moffat so that I could drive to my next gig near Ardrossan. My plan still hinged on the controller working, and there was no way of knowing whether it was ok until the motor was fitted. I had a restful day playing guitar while John re-wired his studio, and after getting packed ready to leave the next morning, I phoned my dad. He sounded more cheerful, as my brother Dave had driven down from Aberdeen to see him, and was staying for a week. I fell asleep thinking about the next leg of my tour, which I'd been looking forward to probably more than any other. If all went to plan, I'd be sailing up the west coast of Scotland in a few days, island hopping from the Mull of Kintyre as far as the Outer Hebrides and the Isle of Skye.

EIGHT

Out at Sea

I GAVE JOHN and Mairi a big hug the next morning before leaving, and John said I was welcome back anytime. Having acclimatised to the Hire Car Dimension, I took the quick route on the motorway back to Henshaw, arriving at the garage by lunchtime. As I drew onto the forecourt my heart lifted as I saw Gary driving Bluebell, but when I parked up and asked him if all was ok, Gary just shook his head and said, 'We've still got problems I'm afraid. She's still not driving properly.'

Gary ran some more tests, and confirmed his fears that the controller had blown. The good news was that the motor was now fixed, but the controller would take two days to be ordered. It would have to be fitted on Thursday, the day I was due to be catching my ferry to the Mull of Kintyre. It would also involve extra costs, not only to fit the controller, but to arrange transport all the way to Ardrossan, where my ferry sailed on Thursday evening. I phoned Willy in Moffat to let him know I wouldn't be able to leave that night, and he said that he couldn't collect me on Thursday as he had another job on. Although I wasn't due to be performing on Kintyre until the Friday night, I had to catch the Thursday ferry as they only ran every two days. Simon, who'd collected Bluebell in his lorry from Once Brewed, said he'd make enquiries for me into the cost of transporting us to Ardrossan.

I thanked Gary for all his efforts, who told me that he'd be away later in the week but would be sending one of his colleagues, Mike, to make sure I was on the road again in time. I now needed to figure out where I was going to stay for the next few nights. The Youth Hostel at Once Brewed was full up, but they suggested trying a hostel at Alston, the lovely market town I'd passed through on my way over the North Pennines. There was no reply when I phoned them, but as Alston was only about 20 miles away, I decided to take my chances and drove up there in the hope that there'd be a bed available for the night. It was a strange feeling back-tracking on the route I'd already driven with Bluebell, but it was a beautiful route, and I pulled over several times to look at the hills, managing to fit my customary nap in along the way.

When I arrived at Alston, the hostel was empty apart from an Italian man and his autistic son. We struck up a conversation in the kitchen, using a mixture of pidgin English (much easier to understand than pigeon!) and sign language, and he told me about the walking holiday they were on. After watching them cook the biggest pan of pasta I've ever seen in my life, I cooked myself some supper, and sat eating it looking out at the trees, which had a family of red squirrels running around in. It brought back fond memories of my childhood home in Formby, which had a red squirrel reserve that my mum used to take my brother and myself to visit every week.

After supper, I went for a walk around Alston and discovered a path along the river that wound its way to the far end of the town. Standing at 1,000 feet above sea level, Alston shares the title of highest market town in England with Buxton in Derbyshire. Historically a mining town, the surrounding area was mined for tin, lead, silver, zinc and coal. The nearby Roman fortress of Whitley Castle was thought to have been built as a way of controlling the income from the lead mines, which were still in operation until the 1950s (although I don't think the Romans were still collecting taxes at that point!). Today, the population of Alston has dwindled to about 1,200, due to a lack of jobs in the area, which now revolve mainly around farming and tourism.

For a small place, Alston certainly had a lot of pubs – I counted eight during my circuit of the town. It was a beautiful summer's evening, and the locals were sitting outside enjoying the sunshine and a tipple, but I suddenly felt very lonely and longed to be home again. When I got back to the hostel the lounge was empty, and I sat watching the squirrels for a while, hoping that tomorrow would bring better news.

I spent the next morning writing a press release to send out to newspapers and radio stations in Scotland. Simon from Henshaw garage phoned to say that he'd spoken with a transport company at Carlisle, who could take Bluebell to Ardrossan for £500. It seemed a lot of money, so I phoned a few other companies and was given quotes almost twice that amount. I told one haulier that I'd been quoted £500, and he replied, 'Well they should have their arm cut off for charging that price', putting the phone down on me. When another lady said, 'I'm afraid we only do kippers' I finally gave up, and phoned Simon back to ask him to book the company from Carlisle.

Fed up with the complexities of tour logistics, I made myself a packed lunch and went for a walk along the Pennine Way. Mossy steps from the hostel led down to the river, and I was soon out into lovely countryside, crossing pretty bridges, and climbing up into the North Pennine hills. Neil, the owner of the hostel, had warned me that there was a grumpy bull in one of the fields, and sure enough as I climbed a stile over a wall, there he stood in the middle of a large field possessively surveying his territory. I tried to avoid eye contact with him, and walked round the edge of the field watching him out of the corner of my eye, for some reason muttering 'Good bull, good bull'. After a while he seemed to lose interest, but even so I was ready to run, until I'd finally climbed a stone wall at the far end of the field.

I found a nice sunny spot with views all around the North Pennines, and sat with my back against a warm wall eating my packed lunch. It was just what I needed after the stress of the last few days, and some lambs came and stood a few yards away watching me inquisitively. I shut my eyes and let myself enjoy the feeling of just being, soaking up the rays of sun and listening to the lambs bleating happily to themselves. Afterwards, I spent a quiet night back at the hostel watching the squirrels again, and chatting with Neil. He said the following night they had a large group of cyclists booked in, and the hostel would be full. Hopefully it would be my last night in England for a while if all went according to plan.

I sent out my press release and photos the next morning to

all the contacts I'd been given by Rob Ellen, the music promoter from the Highlands who I'd been in touch with when I'd been first planning the tour. Rob had been a constant source of encouragement, and phoned me that morning after seeing a post on Facebook saying that Bluebell had broken down.

'How's it going boy?' he enthused. 'You've got this far, you've got to show that milk float who's boss!'

He said that he'd booked me to play at Belladrum festival, one of Scotland's biggest music festivals, where I'd be using Bluebell as an off-grid stage for myself and other performers to play during the festival weekend. It sounded like a lot of fun, and another good reason why I had to keep going on my mission to reach Scotland. I told Rob I'd keep him posted once we were underway again.

Later that afternoon I went for a walk along the North Pennine Way, in the opposite direction to the previous day. I was hoping to find the remains of Whitley Castle, which Neil had told me how to get to, but I managed to get hopelessly lost in the hills. Eventually I came to a farmhouse and asked directions from an elderly lady who was putting washing out in her garden. After carefully surveying the field opposite, she said it should be safe to cross as there were no cattle about, and that I could join a footpath that followed the railway line back into Alston. I stopped in town to get a well needed hair-cut, and returned to the hostel which was now full of cyclists.

Not long after I'd been back, Steve, the walker that I'd made friends with at the hostel in Bellingham, arrived, and we spent the rest of the evening catching up on each other's news.

I needed to be up early the next morning so that I could drop my music equipment off at Henshaw Garage and take the hire car back to Hexham. Hopefully, by the time the hire car company dropped me back again, Bluebell would have her new controller fitted, and the lorry would be there to take Bluebell and myself to Ardrossan, where we'd sail for the Mull of Kintyre that evening.

Mike from EVS was already at Henshaw Garage when I arrived the next morning, and in the process of removing the old controller. He said the new one would be fitted by the time I got back from Hexham, and fingers-crossed Bluebell would be running as normal. When I returned an hour later, Bluebell was on the forecourt with a huge lorry parked next to her, waiting to take us to Ardrossan. Mike came over and said, 'It's all done'.

I was soon back over the border into Scotland again, this time with Bluebell loaded on the back of a lorry. I wished I'd been able to drive her across, but I felt really excited at the thought of being on a Scottish island by that evening. My heart jumped for joy when we reached the signpost for Ardrossan ferry terminal, and just before reaching the port, the driver stopped in a lay-by to unload. It was a while before the ferry was due to leave, so I decided to take Bluebell for a test-run. As soon as I started driving down the road, I knew there was something seriously wrong. She was only driving at half speed, and juddering every few yards as if she were about to stall.

In a panic, I pulled into an Asda car park and phoned Mike up from EVS, who said he'd only driven Bluebell on the garage forecourt, and hadn't been able to drive her at full speed. He was very apologetic, and said he could come first thing the next morning to look at her. I phoned John up from CBL to see if he might have any ideas what the problem could be. He suggested swapping the leads on the motor, so that when I engaged reverse, Bluebell drove forwards instead. This would at least give an idea if the problem was with the motor or the controller. To get to the motor I had to dump all my music gear and bedding on the Asda car park, and soon had a crowd watching as I drove round with Bluebell's reverse alarm blasting out.

I phoned John back, who said that the problem was probably with the controller not the motor, and that it might be something quite simple that could be put right. I needed to make a decision about my ferry route, as I had a chain of tickets that were due to be issued at the CalMac office that day. When I reached the car park at the ferry terminal, the attendant waved me through, saying it would be fine to stay there overnight. The girls at the CalMac office were really helpful and changed my ticket so that I could sail to Arran the following day instead, which would get me back on track for my next gig. I felt really disappointed, though, as I watched the ferry for Campbeltown sail away, and I had to phone the hotel on Kintyre to let them know I wouldn't be coming. I was due to be staying there for two nights with all my food and accommodation paid for, playing on the Friday night in their famous whiskey bar that attracted visitors from all over the world. Instead, I'd be sleeping in a ferry car park and eating at an Asda cafe, such is life on the road!

I went for a long walk along the beach, and sat watching a

family playing with their dog on the sand. I couldn't seem to shake a growing sense of loneliness, and was finding the ups and downs of the tour emotionally exhausting. Grateful for small mercies, I managed to get a reception on my TV when I got back to the ferry car park, and watched a film. Afterwards, I went for another walk, and a huge moon had risen over the sea. I climbed onto the sea wall and stood watching it for a while, a small lighthouse flashing across the water, and the occasional boat sailing into the harbour. I could just about see the outline of Arran in the distance, and I said a little prayer, asking that tomorrow Bluebell and I would be on our way again.

I slept really well that night, and woke the next morning feeling much more positive. After a wash and some breakfast in Asda, I walked back along the beach, with the Atlantic glistening and the Scottish islands looking green and enticing in the distance. Mike phoned not long after to say he was 10 minutes away, and I got all of my gear out of Bluebell and pulled the floorboards up ready for him to inspect the controller. It was the fourth time Tony his apprentice had been out to visit Bluebell, and when they arrived I remarked that he must be sick of the sight of us.

'Not at all', said Tony, 'I think it's amazing what you're doing. I just hope we can get you sorted out'.

Tony and Mike soon had a special device hooked up to the controller, and were taking various readings.

'The settings all look the same as the previous controller', said Mike, 'apart from one of the Modes, which is set to one instead of three. I don't think it will make a difference but we could give it a try'.

Mike made the adjustment, and with Tony standing guard over my gear, we went for a test-run in the ferry terminal car park. As I put my foot down, the familiar whine of the motor kicked in, and Bluebell was suddenly driving at full speed again.

'Good girl Bluebell!' I shouted, barely able to disguise my excitement.

After a couple more laps of the car park, I dropped Mike off so that I could take Bluebell for a proper test-drive, and went in search of the biggest hill I could find. As we climbed up the hill out of town, I was half-expecting Bluebell to start juddering again, but she made it to the top unscathed. We cruised back down the hill at 25mph, and sped through Ardrossan town centre, with surprised onlookers turning to stare as I waved triumphantly at them. I had a huge grin on my face when I got back to the car-park, and thanked Mike and Tony for all their help. After saying our goodbyes, I joined the queue for the Arran ferry, which was due to leave in an hour's time.

It was an exciting feeling driving onto my first ferry, as the CalMac crew gave instructions directing Bluebell into place. I was one of the last vehicles to board, and was guided just inches behind a lorry with barely enough room to open the cab door. The CalMac guys loved Bluebell, and I asked them if a milk float had ever been to the Isle of Arran before, which they thought probably not. It was only a short crossing to Brodick, the main port on Arran, with just enough time to sit up on deck enjoying the view with a tub of Arran ice cream to celebrate. The approach to the island is incredibly beautiful, one side rising high up into the mountains to the east, while the west stretches out low, like a long green dragon's tail.

Brodick had a Mediterranean feel, with palm trees lining the streets, flashy yachts in the harbour, and tourists wandering round the shops in shorts and T-shirts. I was booked at a campsite for a couple of nights in Lamlash, a village about four miles away, and would be returning to Brodick on the Sunday night to stay at the Ormdale Hotel, where I was doing a gig. After stocking up on supplies at the local Co-op, I drove out of town towards my campsite, following a mountain road that led down a steep hill into Lamlash. I was worried that the hill might be too much for Bluebell on our return journey, although I had to find out some time if she was up to the job, as I was pretty sure we had steeper hills to face on the eastern side of Arran, where we'd be travelling to get our next ferry.

Lamlash was a lovely fishing village with a row of traditional cottages running along its main street, and a few shops selling fishing gear, antiquated books and paintings. My campsite was just the other side of the village, and after checking in I cooked some supper, enjoying the view of mountains out of my window. There was a problem hooking up Bluebell to the campsite electrics, which ran on a 10-amp circuit and kept tripping the chargers, but the owner said I could plug into a wall socket in the laundrette the next day instead. I'd also discovered that the inverter connected to my solar panels had blown, which was bad news because I needed it to power my music gear, and relied on it for things like charging up my laptop and phone.

After climbing underneath the floorboards to change the

fuse on the leisure batteries, I found that water had been leaking beneath my carpet into the inverter. Despite changing the fuse a couple of times, each time I tried plugging the inverter in, it just made a horrible bleeping noise, and was evidently broken. In the end I covered the floorboards back over and returned to watching the view out of my window, determined not to let any minor mishaps spoil my day. It was so great to be back in Bluebell again, and I sat for a long time watching the mountains turn a deep orange as night set in, happy that at last I'd made it to the Scottish Isles.

NINE

Arran and Islay

IT WAS COLD and wet the next morning, and after a late breakfast I moved Bluebell round the back of the Laundrette at the campsite to put her on charge. I phoned John from CBL to give him an update, and he said that he'd post me another inverter to a campsite I'd be staying at in Oban in a week's time. He seemed to think Bluebell would be fine now that we'd changed the mode settings on the controller.

'Just watch those hills', he told me. 'Make sure you take plenty of breaks and you'll be fine.'

I was glad of the reassurance, and told him I'd send him a postcard from Edinburgh to let him know I'd arrived safely. About midday I went into Lamlash to try and catch a bus that would take me round the south of the island, but after waiting half an hour or so there was still no sign of it turning up. I got chatting to an elderly lady who was waiting for a bus going in the opposite direction, and she was soon telling me about her son that lived in London, who she was really proud of. I told her about my milk float tour, and just before she got on her bus she said, 'The longest journey…that's the title of your next song.'

I stood for another quarter of an hour waiting for my bus, before getting fed up and walking back to the campsite. My days had been so full and busy recently that I hadn't had any time for songwriting, so I got my guitar out and sat in the back of Bluebell working on the new song title I'd just been given. Later in the afternoon I went for a walk along the beach near the campsite, feeling really at peace as I picked my way across seaweed strewn rocks and bits of driftwood, looking out at Holy Isle opposite.

Its first known name was Inis Shroin, Gaelic for 'Island of the Water Spirit', and was renamed 'Molaise's Island' after a 6th Century Saint, St. Molaise. The son of the King and Queen of Ulster, St. Molaise renounced his entitlement to the throne at the tender age of twenty, and left Ireland in search of enlightenment. It's thought that Holy Isle was already a Celtic spiritual centre when St. Molaise arrived around 586 AD, where he spent the next ten years living in a small cave on the island before departing for Rome and eventually returning to Ireland.

Over the centuries Holy Isle fell into different hands, including Vikings, an American tycoon, and lastly a Mrs Christine Morris, who after being visited in a dream by the Mother Mary, was advised to sell it to a Tibetan Buddhist master, Lama Yeshe. The Mother Mary was evidently a better estate agent than the one who'd sold it to Mrs Morris, as Mrs Morris purchased the island in 1984 for £120,000, and put it up for sale six years later at £1,000,000. After some hard bargaining, however, Lama Yeshe eventually bought it for £350,000, and since then has renovated the buildings to make it into a popular retreat centre.

If I'd had more time, I would have been tempted to spend a few weeks on the island, where you can help out in return for food and board, but I had a strict schedule to stick to if I wanted to make it to Edinburgh by mid-August. I had gigs booked all the way up to the Isle of Harris on the Outer Hebrides, where I'd be joined for a week by a young singer-songwriter called Jade Cuttle, and I also had Daria Kulesh from Folkstock Records meeting me on Skye to play some gigs. After that, I'd be driving to Rob Ellen's hometown of Dingwall, and then playing Belladrum Festival near Loch Ness, before passing Ben Nevis on my way to Perth, and finally Edinburgh.

My confidence was still shaken by my breakdown on Hadrian's Wall, and as I sat looking out at Holy Isle, I wondered what the future was going to bring. It was an incredibly beautiful scene, the ancient island nestled behind a stark red and white lighthouse rising out of the deep blue water. The peace was eventually broken by a couple of razorbills circling overhead, who were making a lot of noise and swooping near my head. I walked back to the campsite and found a leaflet in the information centre advertising live music that night in Brodick, and decided to risk driving Bluebell over the hill into town.

We were soon cruising along Brodick high street, and some revellers in the middle of the road waved me down to ask what I was doing. They were a friendly bunch, and said they'd be along to watch me play the next night at the Ormdale Hotel. The flyer had advertised traditional Scottish music at the bar I was going to, but it turned out be a solo guy playing covers.

The closest it got to traditional Scottish was when he sang Sting's 'Englishman in New York', replacing 'Englishman' with the word 'Scotsman', which the tourist crowd seemed to love. It was nice to be listening to some live music, though, and after staying for a while, I went for a walk along the seafront, which had incredible views over the mountains that I'd be crossing in a few days.

I treated Bluebell to a much-needed wash the next day, and went through all of my gear, separating any essential items from things that I wasn't using. By the end of my clear-out, I'd filled four large boxes ready to send home, and satisfied with my work, I drove back to Brodick in search of the Ormdale Hotel. Trevor the manager was really friendly, and told me how he'd met the landlord's daughter in Glasgow, where they'd both been living at the time. They made the decision to move back to Arran for a quieter life, and hadn't looked back since. Trevor showed me my room and said he'd help me set up for the gig later on, which he was hoping to hold outside in the hotel garden. He seemed to think there'd be quite a few locals along, as there was a jam session in the bar every Sunday night which normally attracted a crowd.

After lunch I went for a walk around the town and discovered more about the local history. With a population of around 4,500, Arran is often described as 'Scotland in miniature' due to being divided by the Highland Boundary Fault that separates the Scottish lowlands from the highlands. Arran's varied fauna flourishes because of its proximity to the Gulf Stream, which prevents frost settling in the winter. Inhabited since the Neolithic period, Arran has a violent and unsettled history, swapping hands from the Gaelic settlers that came from Ireland in the 6th Century, to the Vikings and then the Norwegian monarchy in the 12th Century. Its people were perhaps worst treated by the Scottish aristocracy, most notably Alexander, 10th Duke of Hamilton, who in the 1800s threw almost all the local families off their farms and sent them to Canada with a promise of land that never materialised. The locals' smallholdings were assimilated into large farms belonging to Alexander, resulting in the Gaelic language and culture of the island being virtually destroyed.

Back at the Ormdale Hotel I started setting up in the garden for my evening gig, and Trevor had the bright idea of placing a pair of fans at the back of Bluebell to keep the midges away. It worked a treat, the only problem was that by the time I was ready to play there were no fans of the musical kind, who'd been savaged by the midges and had retreated indoors. The hotel had a beautiful orangery attached to it that was used for diners, and Trevor suggested I move in there instead.

The place was full by the time I started, and some of the locals who'd turned up to play in the jam session came over to introduce themselves. I soon discovered that they weren't really local after all, but English émigrés of the worst kind – folkies. I've met a lot of folkies in my time, and have come to understand there are certain traditions that they feel compelled to follow. These traditions almost always include talking about music as if they know a lot about the subject, accompanied by a desire to not listen to any musicians outside of their own little group. They generally play and sing quite badly, which I suspect is probably why they don't want to listen to anyone else, and in extreme cases there may also be a tankard hanging off a belt!

It was no surprise, then, when they ignored me during the first half of my show, talking loudly from a table just a few yards from me, even when I was introducing my songs. I was standing outside during the interval feeling a bit down-hearted, when a guy who was on holiday came up to me and said, 'Don't worry about those people at the front'. He told me how much he'd enjoyed my music, and that he had great respect for artists who played their own material.

It was enough to spur me on for the second half of the show, realising that if you reach just one person at a gig then it's been worth it. My heart jumped slightly when a couple came in towards the end of the night, one of whom I was pretty sure was the BBC Countryfile series presenter Ellie Harrison. I'd had a bit of a crush on Ellie ever since seeing an episode of Countryfile when she sang a song that she'd written herself. She was just yards from me, and every now and then I'd snatch a glance at her, trying to work out if it was really her or not.

After finishing my second set, I couldn't believe it when Ellie came up to me and said in a broad Scottish accent, 'That was absolutely fantastic'.

'Hang on a minute,' I thought, 'I don't remember Ellie Harrison having a Scottish accent!'

Either the Milk Float Dimension was playing tricks on me, or I'd got Ellie confused with somebody else, and I suspected it was probably the latter. It was still nice to have the affirmation from somebody else who'd enjoyed my music. I sat in the bar afterwards, and Trevor came over to thank me for playing, bringing me a delicious avocado cheese cake. We said our goodbyes, as I had to be away early in the morning to catch a ferry from Lochranza to Claonaig on Kintyre, where I'd be catching another ferry to Islay. Bluebell had only charged part of the day due to problems with the cables tripping, and I waited up until past midnight for the charging lights to turn green. As I reeled the cables in, strains of music wafted from the orangery where the folkies were still at it, and when I say strains, I mean more the sitting on the toilet kind, and as for the wafting...well, I leave that to your imagination!

The sea was translucent blue as I followed the coast road around the island the next morning, the rocky shoreline coming more or less to a stop at the side of the road. Boulders the size of cars stood on the far side of the road, and I counted a huge variety of trees and fauna including beech, pine, palm trees and rhododendrons. I passed the pretty fishing villages of Corrie and Sannox and kept stopping to admire the views, overwhelmed by the untouched beauty of the place. After Sannox the road started gradually climbing, becoming steeper as we ascended into the mountains.

Mindful of John's words of wisdom about taking plenty of breaks on the hills, I pulled over on a mountain pass to give Bluebell a rest, and made some breakfast. I could smell burning from the motor and decided to tackle the remainder of the mountain in short stages, as we still had the steepest section to go. I was surrounded by mist, and it was an eerie feeling being alone with no houses around, and no signal on my phone if I got into trouble. We had a hair-pin bend to negotiate on the final section, but luckily there was nothing coming the other way as Bluebell cornered it on the wrong side of the road in our now well-rehearsed 'Whitfield Bends manoeuvre'. There was an incredible view at the top of the mountain across the valley towards Lochranza, and it was exhilarating free-wheeling down the other side.

The ferry terminal consisted of a small car park leading to the quay, with no ticket office. A few tourists and bikers were gathered outside their vehicles chatting about their different routes through the islands, waiting for the ferry to Claonaig. Unfortunately, I wouldn't be able to explore Kintyre as I had a connecting ferry to catch from Kennacraig to Port Askaig on Islay, and had only an hour to get across a steep mountain range. The ferry crossing only took 30 minutes, and I was soon disembarking towards the next stage of my adventure. A narrow potholed track took us up more mountains, with just the occasional passing place allowing traffic coming the other way to pull over, as Bluebell plodded by at 5mph. Eventually we came to the top of the mountains, and it was all downhill to the ferry terminal at Kennacraig, where we joined the queue for the Islay ferry.

The battery indicator was already flashing red, and I asked one of the CalMac employees if it might be possible to get some charge in Bluebell during the crossing. I was due to be staying on Islay for two nights, playing at the Port Askaig hotel on the second night, and doing some exploring of the island beforehand. It had turned wet and windy, and after getting Bluebell on charge I went upstairs to the ship's lounge to warm up and look at the scenery from the big windows. After about an hour Jura came into view, which lies directly opposite Islay, and I stood on deck for a while watching as we passed her shores. Compared to Islay, Jura is flat and sparse looking, and amongst other things was home to George Orwell for two years while he wrote '1984'.

Seeing Jura shrouded in mist, I could understand how his dystopian novel came to have such a bleak message. I pondered how perhaps Orwell had originally intended to write a light romance, but must have gone off-piste during the long winter months when the lack of daylight could send even the local sheep potty! Islay looked much hillier than Jura, but no less mysterious as we sailed along its coastline towards Port Askaig, passing a half-hidden castle on the cliffs, and a lighthouse flashing next to the harbour.

When I got below deck again the charging cables had both tripped, which meant Bluebell hadn't been able to get any extra charge in her. When I told the CalMac guy, he said, 'Have you seen the hill out of Port Askaig yet? I'd take a good look at it before you decide to go anywhere, especially if your batteries are low.'

I pulled into the car park at the ferry terminal and walked up to the start of the road leading out of Port Askaig, and knew straight away there was no way Bluebell would be able to make it, as the road climbed almost vertically up the cliffs out of the port. I didn't want to spend another night on a ferry terminal carpark, and went to ask at the Port Askaig Hotel if I could stay in return for doing an extra gig. I'd previously been in touch with the owner, a lady called Marianne, who was currently away, and the hotel was being managed in her absence by Mario, a Polish guy in his early 20s. Mario seemed keen on the idea and said he'd phone Marianne, and asked me to wait in reception. Ten minutes later he returned with a big smile on his face and said, 'It's cool. I've spoken to Marianne, and she says you can stay. I'll show you to your room.'

It was a huge rambling hotel, with a dining-room, two bars, and guest rooms spread around upstairs. The guest lounge looked straight over the harbour, and I sat up there for a while watching the small fishing boats coming and going, feeling as if I'd stepped back in time. As I was setting up for my evening gig, I got chatting to some builders who were staying at the hotel while they did some work at a distillery a few miles away. Despite some mild heckling, they were a friendly bunch, and started singing along with one or two cover songs that I played (The Monkee's 'Daydream Believer' went down especially well!). During my second set, I was just about to start a song from my latest album called 'Hard to Admit', when a drunk guy at the bar shouted, 'You've got a nice voice but can you sing something livelier?'

'Yeah, sure', I said. 'This next one's about a man who's thinking of killing himself!'

The rest of the pub laughed at this, and I didn't hear much more from the heckler after that.

I was treated to a huge traditional Scottish breakfast the next morning, and then caught a bus over to Bowmore, the main town on Islay. After climbing the hill out of Port Askaig, the landscape became gently undulating, sparser than Arran but still very pretty, with yellow gauze in full bloom and sheep roaming the hills. I'd never seen such a happy bus in all my life, with the locals all saying hello to each other as they got on and off, and children waving at us from gardens as we passed by. We stopped at a small village called Bridgend, and waited 10 minutes while the driver went off to buy a newspaper, but nobody seemed to mind.

Bowmore has two main streets, with a few shops and fishing cottages leading to the quay, and at its centre is the distillery, a distinctive black and white building with a large stone tower. The air was sweet with the smell of whiskey, and I wondered if this could perhaps be a clue to the contented nature of the locals! Islay has a population of around 3,500, and along with agriculture and tourism, whiskey is its other main industry. At the height of whiskey production there were 23 distilleries on Islay, which is no mean feat considering it's only 25 miles long by 15 miles wide. Alcoholism was a real problem in the past on the island, and workers at the distilleries had to be given four large drams of extra strong whiskey per day to keep them motivated. I wondered what a modern-day health and safety inspector would have made of that!

When I got back to Port Askaig I posted a couple of the boxes I'd packed, and had another huge meal in the hotel restaurant, this time ordering a seafood platter. My plate came piled with lobster, crab, scallops and salmon, with a big bowl of chips and fresh bread. It was the first time I'd eaten lobster, and I had to use a big pair of metal nut-crackers to get the meat out of the claws, scattering bits of shell all over the table and floor in the process. It was hard to get motivated to play my evening gig after such a big meal, but the show must go on, and I went through to the bar to say hello to the builders before I got started. I was just finishing for the night when the man who'd been heckling me the night before came in with a couple of his friends, and said, 'What are you packing your stuff away for? We've come to watch you play!'

He obviously just wanted to heckle me again, and when I told him that I was done for the night he became quite abusive. I had to push past him to get all my gear packed into Bluebell ready to leave in the morning, and was glad to get back to the guest lounge, where I sat for another hour looking out at the harbour. My ferry was already docked for the night, ready to take Bluebell and myself to the tiny island of Colonsay in the morning, where I had a gig booked at the village hall. I sensed it was going to be a special day, and I wasn't to be disappointed.

TEN

Colonsay and Oban

THE SUN WAS shining when I joined the ferry queue the next morning, and it wasn't long before Bluebell was being guided onto the boat by the ever helpful CalMac crew. It was only an hour's crossing to Colonsay, and I stood on the top deck of the ferry at the front of the boat taking in the beauty of my surroundings. We followed the coastline of Islay past the distilleries and lighthouses out into the ocean, sea birds swooping around as the rocky shoreline of Colonsay gradually approached. It was so windy that I had to keep hold of my hat, and the occasional tourist would come out for a photo and then quickly disappear back to the lower decks. I was greeted off the ferry at Colonsay by a man handing out 'What's On' leaflets that included a write-up about my visit to the island.

'You must be the milk float man!' said my enthusiastic tourist guide.

'Yes, the milk float gives it away!' I replied.

I didn't have to go far to reach the village hall, where I was due to be meeting Donald, who'd booked me to perform, and had kindly offered to put me up for the night. I loved Colonsay from the moment I first saw it, with its tiny post office and one shop next to the village hall, which had a boat out the front with children happily playing in it. Donald was waiting for me with a big smile on his face, and we got chatting as he helped me in with my music gear. Donald had lived on Colonsay all his life, and as well as being an accomplished musician was a crofter and also had one or two other jobs on the island, such as doing traffic control at the tiny airport. It sounded an idyllic lifestyle, but I wondered if he ever got bored living in such a small and isolated place.

'Ach, there's too much to do to get bored,' he told me matter-of-factly.

Donald lived with his wife, Carol, in a croft half way round the island that he'd built himself on land inherited from his father. Just ten miles long and two miles wide, Colonsay has a resident population of 135, many of whom Donald hoped would be along to watch me play that night. It was a lovely village hall, with wooden beams that looked like the ribs of a boat, and the acoustics were fantastic. Donald said that Carol was cooking a meal for us later, and as I still had most of the day ahead, I set off in Bluebell to do some exploring on my way to their house.

I wanted to make a video of my day on the island, and wedged my camcorder on a tripod pointing out of the window, grabbing hold of it as Bluebell jolted up and down the potholes in the road. The single-lane track had passing places that every now and then I pulled into to let a car past, and it made me laugh when a car stopped and the driver said, 'See you tonight,' and drove off again without a further word! I carried on past small tracks leading off to crofts nestled in fields full of summer flowers, and eventually came to the top of a hill revealing the ocean beyond. The beaches on Colonsay are incredible, white sands surrounded by cliffs with the wide Atlantic Ocean rolling onto their shore. Donald had suggested stopping at a beach in Kiloran Bay at the top of the island, which I came to after Bluebell climbed a steep hill. I was just brewing up a cup of tea and admiring the view, when a young guy on a three-wheeled bicycle with a sail attached pulled up.

'What are you up to?' I asked him inquisitively.

'I've just cycled from Gloucestershire,' he told me. 'I live on the island, but every now and then I like to go off on an adventure!'

'So how many miles a day can you do on that thing?' I couldn't help but ask him.

'About 30 miles with a good wind.'

'Same here!' I replied.

Cyclists were always interesting to pass in Bluebell, especially uphill, as they very often wouldn't hear me coming. A look of surprise would appear on their faces as I pulled alongside them, barely nudging past at one or two miles per hour faster. Things would get tricky if a car was approaching in the other direction, as I had no way of accelerating past. My usual tactic was to just keep going and hope for the best, which seemed to have worked so far, although I suspected some of the cyclists I'd left wobbling on the side of the road may not have agreed with me!

After doing some filming on the beach I had a nice nap in the back of Bluebell, and then set off for Donald's house. He hadn't told me the address, but just said to follow the road around the island until I came to a long green barn on the left-hand side of the road, with a sign-post pointing towards their croft. It was easy enough to find, and Bluebell bumped down a long track, causing the resident sheep to run for cover as we approached. I felt immediately at home when Duncan invited me in and introduced me to Carol, and we sat drinking tea and chatting for a while looking out at the ocean. Carol had first come to Colonsay to spend a summer working as a student, where she met and fell in love with Donald. After training to become a teacher, she'd spent her working life as the school's main teacher, and was now enjoying early retirement.

It was a beautiful ride to the village hall that evening, with the sun low in the water as Bluebell passed remote fishing cottages on the way. There was a good turnout of locals at the hall, and when they were all seated Donald stood up to introduce me.

'I don't think there's much to be said about a man who comes all the way from Norfolk to Colonsay in a milk float. Sufficient to say he conked out more than once, and it's by tremendous effort that he's arrived to perform for us to-day…please give a big welcome to Paul Thompson'.

After the applause died down, I launched into my first set, playing a collection of old songs and new. It was nice performing to such an appreciative audience, who I got chatting to during the interval. The two people that had stopped earlier in the car came to say hello, and I had a long conversation with an English lady who suffered from MS, and had been living on the island for almost 30 years. Many of the people now living on Colonsay were 'in-comers', which the locals encouraged because the young tended to want to leave. For a small island

Colonsay has a thriving arts scene, with an annual music festival and a literary festival that attracts big names like Alexander McCall Smith and Liz Lochead. I felt it must take a special kind of person to live in such a place, when the winters are bleak and long, but everyone I spoke to seemed very contented with their life on the island.

I spent some time signing CDs after the gig, and once everybody was gone Donald helped me pack away and put Bluebell on charge. We had to feed my cables through a high window into the hall, which Donald hooked over some bins so that sheep wouldn't get tangled up in the wires. The drive home in Carol and Donald's car was magical, the ocean luminescent in the midsummer night, and the occasional fishing boat bobbing on the water. Like the sea, the mountains changed colour constantly, and turned from an orange hue into deep velvet. We sat up for a while chatting when we got back, and Donald told me more about his life on the island, which he said had its ups and downs just like any other place. I especially liked the sound of his part-time job as traffic controller at the airport, and fell asleep imagining what the traffic-control conversations must have sounded like:

'Colonsay International to Air Scotland. Sheep are clear of runway. Please proceed. Over!'

'Air Scotland to Colonsay, could you also please confirm the cow pats are now safely removed. Over.'

'Cow pats dealt with by squadron of wheel-barrows. Over.'

'Roger to that! Coming in to land. Over!'

The next morning Carol told me that she'd heard on the radio that CalMac were planning a strike on the day that I was due to be catching a ferry from Oban to the Outer Hebrides. This was bad news as I had several gigs booked, with a tight schedule to get from one place to the next. The only available ferry was the day after the strike, so I changed my ferry tickets and phoned up the venues to see if I could rearrange the dates. I'd been in touch on Facebook a few months previously with a lady from the Isle of Harris called Grannie Annie, who'd said I was welcome to stay with her in Leverburgh, and when I told her about the problems I was having due to the strike, she said I could visit for as long as I wanted. It was very kind of her, and would take some of the worry out of accommodation arrangements for myself and Jade later in the week.

Around mid-morning Carol said she had to drive into Scalasaig and could give me a lift. I said goodbye to Donald, who was busy testing out a smart new tractor that he'd had imported from India. He'd made me so welcome, and I told him that I hoped I might have the chance to return his hospitality one day. When we arrived at the village hall, I found an envelope taped to Bluebell's windscreen with 'Paul' written on it. A note inside it from a lady called Jane said that she'd enjoyed listening to my music the night before, and had wanted to buy a CD, but didn't have enough cash on her. At the bottom of the envelope was a ten-pound note, and instructions to leave a CD in the post office for her to pick up later. It was a very touching gesture, and typical of the honesty that I'd found on Colonsay. I dropped the CD in at the post office, and the post master helped me wrap up another box that I wanted to send home. Carol was busy working in the community garden next to the hall, and waved me off as I drove Bluebell up to the quay to wait for my ferry.

It was a spectacular journey to Oban, following the green cliffs of Mull on the way into Oban's imposing harbour. Oban was much bigger than I'd expected, with large Victorian style hotels lining the waterfront and a busy metropolitan buzz about the place. After the peace and quiet of Islay and Colonsay, I found it almost too much, and after a quick foray into the town centre, I turned Bluebell around and headed for our campsite about three miles away. When I'd spoken to the owner, I'd asked if there were any big hills on the way, and she'd said it was ok except for a bit of a slope from the road up to the site. I looked in horror as we approached the turning, with a massive hill rising at a 45 degree angle, but after a couple of run-ups Bluebell just made it to the top.

My inverter had arrived from CBL and I spent the afternoon carefully fitting it. As I attached the final wire I prepared for the worst, expecting a loud bang, but amazingly when I plugged my small TV in everything was working. I improvised a meal of baked potato with macaroni cheese and salami to celebrate, and afterwards went for a walk on the road leading up a hill from the campsite. The views were incredible, looking across several valleys towards Oban and the ocean in the distance. I reached a private estate and was just turning around when I heard footsteps quickly approaching, and a teenage boy ran up to me and said accusingly, 'Have you just come from in there?'

'No,' I replied defensively, 'I'm staying at the camp site down the road.'

'Oh, that's alright then. I thought you might have been a

poacher,' he said, and ran off as quickly as he'd arrived. Poaching wasn't really my scene, and anyway I didn't have a suitable getaway vehicle!

The next day, I heard that the CalMac strike had been called off, which meant I could catch the ferry with Jade the following morning as originally planned. It was still a logistical nightmare, though, because when I phoned round the venues to re-arrange the original gig dates, some of them now said they wanted to keep the new date that we'd agreed upon. I was due to be picking Jade up in Oban that afternoon, where we'd be driving to a venue called the Barn Bar about six miles away. The plan was to return to Oban after the gig and join the queue ready for our ferry early the next morning to South Uist, where we'd be staying and performing at the Lochboisdale Hotel on the Saturday night.

I hadn't appreciated the beauty of Oban the first time I ventured into the town, and spent the afternoon wandering round its independent shops and pretty waterfront. I just had time to post my final parcel home before meeting Jade off her train. After stopping in a cafe, we loaded her things into Bluebell and set off for the Barn Bar in Cologin. Danny, the owner, was a DJ on Oban FM and had been plugging the gig for the last week, and was expecting a good turnout. One of the regulars there, a man called Liam, had been sending me enthusiastic emails saying how fantastic he thought it was that I was travelling in a milk float, and I was looking forward to meeting him as he sounded quite a character.

The road out of Oban towards Cologin was incredibly steep, and I had to zigzag to keep Bluebell's speed up. I think

Jade was wondering what she'd got herself into, but we were soon out into rolling countryside and followed a narrow track down to the Barn Bar, which was at the end of the road in a fern-covered valley. It was a beautiful place to play for the night, a rustic-looking barn with a veranda out the front with a wood-burning stove. We were made really welcome by Danny, who said we could have whatever we wanted to eat, and after a lovely fish pie, Jade and I sat in Bluebell for a while drinking tea before setting up for the evening gig.

Liam came in just before Jade started playing and introduced himself with a big smile on his face. He was in his mid-60s, and had a very contented look about him, which I guessed may have been aided by the occasional tipple. Liam apologised in advance for his bad singing which he said he was prone to breaking into at any given moment, and I told him I'd play some requests for him. After I'd finished my set, I sat chatting with Liam and his friends for a while until the conversation turned to politics, at which point I beat a hasty retreat outside. Jade was sitting with Danny and a few others who'd lit the wood-burner and had been knocking back plenty of drinks.

'Have you heard about the famous hill out of Tarbert yet?' Danny asked me.

Actually, I had, because somebody on Facebook had been posting comments about how I was going to be stuck in Harris for a long time due to the hill in question. Danny said he'd ask his father who lived in Tarbert if he could tow me up the hill, which sounded like it might be our only option if we wanted to reach the Isle of Lewis.

ELEVEN

The Outer Hebrides

It was 2am by the time we arrived at the ferry port in Oban, and I was so tired that I just found the first lane I could, and parked Bluebell, hoping we were in the right place to catch our ferry to South Uist in a few hours. I woke again at 6am to the sound of walkie-talkies, and when I looked out of the window a queue of cars was behind us. It turned out we were in the wrong lane, and had been holding everyone up. Eventually I found the lane for the South Uist ferry, and woke Jade up who was still asleep in the back of Bluebell.

I felt really drained from the previous night, and after driving onto the ferry went in search of some breakfast. This turned out to be a big mistake, as not long afterwards we were out into a choppy ocean and I started to feel sick. Lying down in the ship's lounge only made things worse, and I spent the next half an hour in the toilets throwing up. Afterwards I made my way back to the lounge feeling sorry for myself, and fell asleep for almost two hours. When I woke again, we were approaching Lochboisdale on South Uist, and I felt really annoyed with myself for having missed the journey.

South Uist is one of the largest Hebridean Islands, joined to

North Uist by Benbecula, a tiny land mass in between. The Uists lie just above Barra, the bottom most of the Outer Hebridean Isles, which I'd visited on holiday a few years before. I'd had a wonderful couple of days staying in a small B+B with my brother and his family, hiring bikes to cycle round the island and doing some canoeing. It gave me a taste for the Hebrides that had made me want to come back, but I never would have guessed that I'd be returning in a milk float.

The hills surrounding Lochboisdale were covered in mist and drizzle, and the village looked sparse with just a small shop, a few houses, and the Lochboisdale Hotel, where we were staying for the night. Karen the owner was very welcoming, and more than made up for the cold and damp weather. Originally from Yorkshire, she and her husband had visited the island on holiday and fallen in love with the place, making the brave move to sell up their house and start a new life. It seemed to be working well for them, as the hotel was full. The Uists attract visitors from all over the world, who come to fish its small sea lochs (known as lochans), where wild trout and salmon are abundant.

After getting Bluebell on charge I went for a lie down in my hotel room as I was still feeling sick from the ferry journey. My throat was hurting and I wasn't sure whether I'd be well enough to play that night, but after a good meal I felt much better by the time I was due to start. During the break a man came over to say hello who was originally from Ipswich, but was now living on the Isle of Skye. He'd sailed over from Skye in his boat to watch me play, and we ended up talking about the various footballing fortunes of Norwich City and Ipswich town.

I felt revitalised the next morning after a good night's sleep, and South Uist looked a different place in the bright sunshine. There was no rush to get away, as we were travelling about 25 miles that day, crossing Benbecula and stopping at a campsite on the southern tip of North Uist. We made our way gradually through the island, passing beautiful lochans full of water-lilies bordered by wild roses and heather-clad moors. There were no villages in sight, just the occasional pebbledash cottage, and we stopped to take a photo of Jade standing next to a road-sign with 'Caution Otters Crossing' written on it.

Eventually, a long bridge took us across tidal mud-flats to Benbecula, which had a Co-op store that surely must be a contender for 'Supermarket with the Most Beautiful View in Britain Award.' It made my day when I spotted a write-up about my tour in the Sunday Post, who I'd done an interview for by telephone on Islay earlier that week. It had a big picture of me standing in front of Bluebell with my guitar, and the headline, 'A Great Adventure – and Paul's Milking It!'.

After getting stocked up on supplies for the next few days, we crossed the bridge from Benbecula onto North Uist, and not long after came to the turning for Moorcroft Farm, where we were staying. I was so pre-occupied looking at the incredible views out to sea that I managed to drive Bluebell into a soft verge and got her front wheel stuck in the mud. I tried reversing out, but was worried that I might damage the motor, and ran to the campsite to see if anyone could help. There was soon a group of five or six people pushing Bluebell, but she wouldn't budge.

In the end I had to go back to the farmhouse and explain to

the farmer how I'd managed to drive a milk float into the side of his ditch. Luckily, he saw the funny side of it, and towed Bluebell out with his 4x4 truck. After parking up on the campsite, I helped Jade set up her tent, and it was so windy that we both had to hold onto it as we pegged it down. Jade said she wanted to go off to do some filming for her blog, and I took the opportunity to do some more exploring of my own, following the main road towards a row of houses in the distance that led down to the beach.

I'd been walking a mile or so when a procession of about 30 massive army trucks rattled past, with soldiers waving as they went by. Uist was used as an army missile base during the 1950s, when despite opposition from the locals, it housed nuclear weapons that formed an important strategic element in the Cold War with Russia. I couldn't imagine a more peaceful place to hold such a destructive thing, and apparently the explosions from the test launches were heard throughout the island.

I took a detour on the way back to the campsite over some peat bogs, and soon found out why the campsite owner had warned me not to stray too far off the road. The path was incredibly squelchy and I was plastered in mud by the time I found my way back to the campsite. I'd worked up quite an appetite, and cooked supper for myself and Jade in a lovely old stone bunkhouse that had been converted into a kitchen. Even though it was mid-summer the evenings were chilly, and after our meal I went back to Bluebell and climbed in my sleeping bag to keep warm, looking out at the mud flats turning into a myriad of colours as the tide receded.

I woke up early the next morning and spent some time catching up on tour emails, and then had to get organised for the journey to Berneray, where we were catching a ferry later that day to the Isle of Harris. There was no sign of Jade, who'd been up late doing her blog, and was still asleep in her tent. I felt a bit like a schoolteacher telling her that we needed to get ready to leave, hurrying her along as we packed the tent away. We stopped in Lochmaddy to give Bluebell a break, and had a wander round the tiny town. It made me laugh when I spotted the bank, which was just a bungalow with a 'Bank of Scotland' sign above it. If somebody wanted to rob the place, they wouldn't have to spend much time working out a plan.

'It should be easy enough Jack…Mrs MacDonald normally keeps a spare key under the front doormat, and the money's in a vase in the kitchen!'

I couldn't imagine that crime would be much of a problem on the island, though. Uist reminded me of an island in Alaska called Seldovia, where I'd been hosted by a local family during a folk festival that I was performing at. When the family kindly offered me the use of their car for the weekend, I asked why they left the key in the ignition.

'Oh, we don't have any crime here,' one of my hosts told me. 'We used to have a blind policeman, and when he retired we just didn't bother getting another one!'

After Lochmaddy, the landscape became gradually hillier and wilder as we approached the top of the island. Berneray is joined to North Uist by a long causeway, and it felt utterly surreal driving across it in Bluebell with not a house in sight, surrounded by marshland, mountains and endless views across the Atlantic Ocean. There was just a small car park at the ferry terminal, and after joining the queue a lady came up to me and said, 'Hello Paul. I'm Susy MacCauley from the Islands News and Advertiser.'

I'd been in touch with Susy several months prior to the tour starting, and had done a couple of phone interviews for her paper. It was lovely to put a face to the voice, and we did another interview so that Susy could give her readers an update. The ferry ride across the Sound of Harris was spectacular, with the cliffs of Harris ahead, and small rocky outposts in between, which the ferry had to weave in and out of by steering through giant buoys. I watched transfixed as the little white houses on the shores of Leverburgh came gradually into view, feeling as if I were in another world.

We were due to be staying at Grannie Annie's that night, and she'd given me instructions on how to find her house at Rodel, which was a couple of miles out of Leverburgh. After leaving the ferry, we followed a road up a deep gorge, passing sheep on the side of the road who watched us inquisitively as I shouted words of encouragement to Bluebell. Suddenly we were at the top of a lush valley that reminded me of a scene out of Lord of the Rings. Streams ran down the sides of the mountain into lochs, and an ancient looking church stood on the horizon with the ocean behind it. Annie's house was just past the ridge of the hill, with fantastic views down towards the village. When I knocked on the door, Annie's husband, Rob, appeared in a pinny.

'Annie's at work,' he explained, 'and I'm in the middle of preparing us a meal for tonight. Come in.' I was touched by

Rob's kindness in making us so welcome. After getting settled in, I went for a walk into Rodel to do some exploring. The church of St Clements looked like a small castle, with three levels and a tiny stone staircase that wound up to a turret at the top with views over the cliffs. As I walked back down, I got quite a shock as a family had come in while I was up there, and their teenage son shouted 'Aghhh' at the top of his voice to test the acoustics!

Rob was sitting outside when I got back, and we made the most of the sunshine while Toby their black spaniel had fun running around the garden. Annie arrived back not long afterwards from Tarbert, where she worked in a Harris tweed shop. It was interesting hearing about her and Rob's lifestyle change that had taken them from good jobs in Cardiff to a more uncertain future on Harris. After some initial hardships they were now doing really well renting their annexe out as a holiday home, which gave them a good income combined with Annie's job at the Harris tweed shop.

After eating the delicious Chinese stir-fry meal that Rob had cooked, Annie said that she'd take Jade and me in her car to Tarbert so that I could check out the hills that we'd be crossing in a few days. Annie's enthusiasm and knowledge about Harris was infectious, and she could easily have made a living from being a tour guide, as she knew so much about the geology and history of the islands. She pointed out long crevices in the mountainsides that had been gorged by the locals dragging seaweed up off the beach to dry out in days gone by, when times were so hard during the Clearances they were forced to eat the seaweed to survive.

Harris has one of the most incredible landscapes I've ever seen, constantly changing from wide Atlantic views to swathes of fertile moorland called macchair, full of native wild flowers such as Lady's Bedstraw, corn marigolds, orchids and bog-cotton. As we drove further up into the mountains the landscape changed again, passing weirdly shaped boulders that looked so strange they were used for scenes in the film '2001: A Space Odyssey'. There was no way Bluebell would be able to make it to the top of the mountain range, and Annie said the infamous hill the other side of Tarbert was even steeper and longer than the one we were on.

It was a real problem, because as well as needing to get to our gig in Tarbert, we were due to be catching a ferry to Skye from there in a week's time. After driving around Tarbert we stopped at one of Annie's favourite beaches in a place called Luskentyre. It was a magical scene as the sun set on the mountains with an incredible rainbow aura around them, the white sands changing purple in the fading light while we threw sticks out to sea for Toby to fetch.

The next morning I walked into Leverburgh with Rob to get some supplies, while Toby ran wild up and down the mountainsides. The Co-op store at Leverburgh had a lochan at the front, which Toby swam in while Rob was in the shop, and some local children threw stones for him to chase. As we'd forgotten Toby's lead, I had to hold onto him until Rob came out again, by which time I was soaked through and smelling of dog and river water! On the way back I stopped in at the Post Office and bought a wonderful book called 'Crowdie and Cream', an autobiography of a writer called Finlay J. Mac-

Donald who'd grown up near Rodel at the turn of the 20th Century. It told of his upbringing in a croft, that despite having outdoor toilets, no electricity or running water, was a fertile playground of the imagination for a young boy growing into adulthood. Interestingly, it recounted an incident in St. Clement's church where the author had encountered a dark and unnatural presence. I wondered if this could be the same phantasm that shouted 'Aghhh!' at me while I was in there, although I wasn't sure that ghosts normally wear Nike trainers!

Rob told me more about the history of Harris on our way back to the house. Until 1920 Leverburgh had been called Obbe, but had been bought by William Lever, aka Viscount Leverhulme, who'd first visited the islands and fallen in love with them in his early 30s, many years later buying the South Harris Estate for £36,000. His plan was to turn the area into a major fishing port, and he did a lot to improve the local infrastructure such as rebuilding the roads and harbour. The changes were welcomed by the locals, as it generated much needed income for them, but sadly Viscount Leverhulme was taken ill on a trip to Africa and suddenly died. The executors of his estate had no interest in the project, funds were withdrawn and the village again fell into disrepair after being sold for £5,000. Today the main industries in Leverburgh are fishing and tourism.

Later that day I took Bluebell for a spin and did some filming, stopping to go for a walk past a lochan with a beautiful white clapboard house in front of it. A path beyond it led up to the cliffs, and I stood for a while gazing in awe across the small islands lying between the Sound of Harris and Skye. On the way back to Annie and Rob's I got a phone call from The Sun newspaper, and pulled over at a passing place at the top of the valley.

'So where are you now?' Anna the journalist asked me.

'Actually, I'm sitting on top of a mountain in my milk float', I replied.

'Oh wow!', said Anna.

'So am I going to be on Page Three?' I couldn't help but ask. Anna laughed, and said she thought her readers would love the story of my journey. For a Sun journalist she seemed much more intelligent than I might have expected, and she was genuinely interested in my journey. She said she'd let me know when the article would be published, and although The Sun would be just about the last newspaper I'd normally buy, it was still a good thing that I'd be getting some extra publicity.

Afterwards, I managed to get Bluebell's front wheel stuck in Rob and Annie's lawn after doing a reversing manoeuvre that went slightly askew. I asked Rob if he'd give me a hand pushing Bluebell out again, and the lawn was soon covered with bits of carpet, planks of wood and rocks that we jammed beneath the wheel. Much as we tried pushing, pulling, rocking forwards and backwards, Bluebell wouldn't budge, and despite being very nice about it, I could tell Rob was getting fed up with the gaping chasm that was opening up on their newly laid lawn.

I'd spotted a breakdown recovery van at a house down the road earlier that day, and I ran down to it to see if anyone could help tow me out. The owner's daughter came to the door and said her dad was at work in Leverburgh, but she phoned him up and said he could be there in ten minutes. He arrived just as I got back to the house, and for the bargain price of £10 attached a rope to his van and pulled Bluebell out in one go. The hole in the lawn looked awful, though, and I dreaded what Annie would think when she got back the following day from a family wedding she'd gone to in Cardiff.

Rob told me not to worry about it, and said he was going to cook some supper for myself and Jade. While Rob was in the kitchen, I got chatting to some guests staying in the annexe, who by a strange coincidence were from Norfolk.

'So how long did it take you to get here?' I asked them.

'Oh, just a day. We flew from Norwich and hired a car. How about you?'

'Oh, about six weeks give or take a day or two!' I told them.

Talking about Norfolk made me homesick, and I phoned my dad to see how he was. He'd now been given another date for his operation in early August, just before his birthday. We normally had a combined celebration, as my birthday is the week after his, and I told him that we'd do something special together when I got back. Rob cooked Jade and me a delicious lamb and sweet potato curry, and I'd bought some mixed berries and ice cream from the Co-op which we had for pudding. Rob and I decided that Jade needed educating in some classic comedy, and we watched 'Monty Python's Meaning of Life', followed by 'Spinal Tap'. I tried to think what a 'mockumentary' of my own tour might be like – and realised I was actually living it!

TWELVE

Back the Way We Came

I TRIED TO catch up on tour emails the next morning, but kept getting distracted by the gorgeous view out of Rob and Annie's huge kitchen window. I was still making arrangements for the Edinburgh Fringe, where I was due to be arriving the second week of August, performing for two weeks on George Street. I'd booked myself and Bluebell onto a campsite at the Royal Highland Centre near Edinburgh airport, which looked really nice, but the location worried me slightly because the only way into the city centre was on a busy A-road. I also had some financial worries that needed sorting out, as there was a big bill to pay for the repairs on Bluebell. My brother, Dave, had said that if I needed to borrow some more money I could, and although I didn't like asking him, I couldn't see any other option. I sent him an email, and within half an hour had a reply saying, 'Yes, no problem, I'll put the money in your account later today'.

After lunch Jade and I went for a run along the coast road in Bluebell, and we parked next to a beautiful beach, playing guitar and drinking tea for the afternoon. We had a gig to get to that evening, at a seafood restaurant in Leverburgh called

The Anchorage. On our way back to town we stopped at the Co-op and I got chatting to the local milkman in the car park, who was highly amused when I told him about my journey. He used a diesel van to do his rounds, and when I suggested he gave it a try in Bluebell instead, he said, 'Och...I'd probably get the sack as I'm late enough everywhere I go already!'.

After taking some photos with the milkman, Jade and I headed off to The Anchorage for our gig. It was a lovely restaurant right next to the harbour, and Sally the owner welcomed us in and showed us to a table. I'd arranged a fee for the night that included a meal for myself and Jade, but when it came to ordering, Jade said in a loud voice, 'I might as well have the lobster as it's free'. I'd asked for a steak, and between us we'd managed to order the two most expensive items on the menu. I think the waitress overheard Jade's comment, because Sally came over not long afterwards and said, 'I'm really sorry, but you've ordered over £70 worth of food. Could you either pay something towards it or order something else instead?' I was absolutely mortified, and we hastily re-ordered fish and chips. It wasn't a good start to the night!

The bar was filling up nicely with locals while I set up for the gig, but a man who looked like he'd been drinking all afternoon kept talking gibberish at me. During my opening set he stood up and started singing along, sounding like he was wailing in pain. After being reprimanded by the bar staff he sat down for a while, but when Jade started playing, he really let rip. I felt sorry for Jade, as the man was standing right in front of her, making it really difficult for her to perform. It got so bad that in the end the bar staff had to forcibly remove him from the pub, which resulted in a shouting match outside before he eventually disappeared home. Sally came through from the restaurant during my final set as I was telling some stories from my tour, and she was soon laughing along with the rest of the pub. I got Jade up on stage to play the last song, and we finished with an encore.

Even though I'd drunk nothing stronger than Coke that night, I felt really groggy when I woke up the next morning, and went for a walk to try and clear my head. It was a lovely summer's day, and I stopped at the Co-op to buy a picnic for the walk back. I was starting to appreciate the gentle sense of humour that the islanders have, and when I asked the man behind the counter at the Co-op if he knew of a nice way to walk back to Rodel, he said, 'Hang on I'll get my map out, it makes me feel very important you know!'

He showed me a coastal path that followed the road until it reached a big hill that led across the cliffs to Rodel. Armed with my picnic supplies I set off on the coast road, stopping every now and then to look at the boats anchored in the little bays. I peered inquisitively at the cottages along the way, with fishing nets, lobster pots and old cars lying about their gardens. It made me laugh when a flock of sheep in front of one cottage were shooed away by an elderly lady who shouted, 'Dirty little creatures' after them as they went. At the end of the road was an extraordinary garden with a couple of whitewashed outhouses, amongst a huge array of flowers in stone containers covered in sea-shells. I wondered who tended it as there were no houses in sight, but it was obviously very well cared for.

The path rose up over the cliffs, and I stopped at the top for a lunch of chicken pie, an apple, a chocolate bar and a can of lemonade. I felt truly in heaven sitting there with my picnic looking out at the Isle of Skye in the distance. I certainly ate well that day, as Rob was preparing a huge lasagne for us all when I got back later in the afternoon. Annie returned from her trip to Cardiff full of stories about her daughter's wedding, but didn't say anything about the hole in the lawn, which she'd already seen as Rob had posted a photo of it on Facebook. I sensed that perhaps it was time to start making plans for our departure, though, as Rob and Annie had been so generous, and I hated the thought of out-staying our welcome.

I phoned CalMac the next morning, and there was space on a ferry sailing the following day from Lochmaddy to Uig, on the Isle of Skye. The ferry didn't leave until mid-afternoon, which would give us just enough time to get across from Leverburgh to North Uist, and then drive back the way we'd come to Lochmaddy. I spent my final day on Harris doing some more filming with Bluebell, and when it started raining in the afternoon, drove along the coast road and sat with my guitar looking out at the stormy ocean, working on some ideas for a new song. Bluebell's front cab was perfect for songwriting as there was plenty of space for my guitar, the acoustics sounded great, and I had a widescreen view through the window to inspire me.

With most of a new song written, I drove back to Annie and Rob's, and after doing some packing ready for leaving the next day, I went to get us all some fish and chips. We spent the rest of the night chatting, and when I told Annie and Rob about the distance I'd still got to travel during the remainder of my tour, Annie said, 'Why don't you apply for a Guinness World Record?' It wasn't something I'd even thought about until she suggested it, and I looked on the Guinness World Records website to see if there was a current record for the longest journey by milk float. I found a record for the fastest milk float, but there didn't appear to be a current record for the longest journey. I filled in an online application on the Guinness World Records website, giving them as much information about my tour as I could. I'd worked out that I'd be travelling roughly 1,500 miles, not including the ferry journeys. If my record attempt was successful, it would take any contenders a long time to beat!

It was cold and wet the next morning as Jade and I said our goodbyes to Annie and Rob. 'No need to invite yourselves over next time,' said Annie. 'Just let us know when you're on the ferry!' I was excited at the thought of travelling to the Isle of Skye, which I'd visited on holiday a couple of years previously. I remembered that there was a very steep hill out of Uig, where we'd be staying that night, and I hoped that Bluebell would be able to get up it. Skye had the steepest hills of the tour so far, and I'd carefully gone over my route with the gradient website I was using. There were only two ways to get from Uig round the island, one was really hilly, and the other was really, really hilly. I decided on the really hilly route!

After taking the ferry back across the Sound of Harris, we retraced our route over the causeway from Berneray to North Uist. It was a wild day and the wind was blowing Bluebell around the road as we drove towards Lochmaddy. The doors of the cab had gaps in them that would blow the cold air straight in, and Jade and I were wrapped up in jumpers, coats and woolly hats to keep warm. We arrived at Lochmaddy in plenty of time for our ferry, and sat in the back of Bluebell drinking tea and sheltering from the cold. The journey to Skye only took an hour or so, and we couldn't see very much as a thick mist had descended on the water. I wondered if the weather had been like this when Flora MacDonald rowed Bonnie Prince Charlie from Benbecula across to Skye, in the legend that became 'The Skye Boat Song'.

The story goes that Flora MacDonald was living on Benbecula during the Jacobite Risings, when in June 1746 Bonnie Prince Charlie took shelter at her house after escaping the Battle of Culloden. Flora offered to help Prince Charlie escape, disguising him as a maid after gaining permission to cross from Benbecula to Skye in a boat with six rowers. They were refused entry to Skye at Waternish, but were eventually allowed to land at Kilbride, where Flora MacDonald hid Prince Charlie amongst rocks until she was able to arrange for him to be transported to the main town of Portree.

Flora was later arrested and tried in London for her part in his escape, and imprisoned in the Tower of London. She was granted a reprieve in 1747 after marrying a captain in the army, and emigrated to America. Her story was an eventful one, as in 1749 her husband was killed in the American Revolution, and she returned to Skye. On the way back she was stopped by privateers and injured whilst putting up a fight, but eventually made it home, and spent the remainder of her days at Dunvegan, and later Kingsburgh, where she died peacefully in 1790 at the age of 68.

It was still misty and wet when we reached our campsite at Uist, and the rain had made the grass on the campsite really soggy. After skidding around for a while in Bluebell and pitching Jade's tent, we went for a meal at a café to warm up, and had a walk around Uig, which apart from a few houses and the harbour area, didn't have much else. I kept looking at the hill that we'd be driving up the next morning, wondering if it would be too steep for Bluebell. There was a U-bend halfway that appeared to be even worse than the one we'd cornered on the 'Whitfield Bends'. But we now had a Guinness World Record to aim for, and if there was any milk float in the country up to the job, I knew it was Bluebell!

The clouds had cleared the next morning as we set off on the hill out of Uig towards Staffin Bay. Once we'd started on the hill, there was no way I could stop if Bluebell was going to reach the top. Jade looked horrified as we cornered the U-bend, just as another driver managed to swerve out of the way. We made it to the top, though, and followed the coast road around the north of the island, passing some dramatic scenery with tall granite cliffs on one side of us, and the ocean crashing against a rocky shoreline below. The road was incredibly hilly, and we made several stops on the way to let Bluebell cool down, which also gave us a chance to do some sightseeing. We had a look round the ruins of Duntulum Castle, right at the northern tip of Skye, and it was exhilarating standing on the lichen-covered rocks with the ocean crashing around us as cormorants circled overhead.

Later that night at the campsite I cooked a meal for us, and afterwards went for a walk. Skye really is incredibly beautiful, with white cottages peppering its coastline, and spectacular hills constantly changing colour and texture. The fields were full of buttercups, purple clover and long grasses silhouetted in the late evening sun, and I followed a small road to a deserted cottage where I sat watching the sun set over the mountains.

We had some free time to explore the island the next day, and set off in Bluebell for the Quiraing hills. We were heading for a car park at the foot of the hills, but the road up to it was really steep and narrow, with only room in places for one vehicle to pass. About halfway up, a car driving towards us stopped, and as I tried to get past I heard a bump at the back of Bluebell. I didn't think anything of it, and carried on up the road. It was too steep for us to get all the way up to the car park, so we stopped after another mile at a lay-by, and were just getting out of Bluebell when a car pulled over, and a man jumped out, shouting, 'You've just trashed the side of my car. I can't believe you didn't stop.'

'I'd no idea I hit you,' I replied, trying to look as innocent as I could.

Bluebell's rear wheel-arch had been scraped, but there was no other damage I could see. Eventually the man calmed down after I gave him my insurance details, assuring him that I'd accept responsibility for the incident. It had turned wet and windy by the time Jade and I reached our footpath up to the top of the Quiraing Hills, and I was feeling shaken after my altercation with the man. The last time I'd come up here it had been sunny and the hills were full of bluebells as far as the eye could see, but when Jade and I stopped for our packed lunch, we could only see a few yards ahead of us. The rain had made the path too slippery to continue the way we were going, so we turned around and drove back to the campsite to dry out. I had a phone interview to do that afternoon with Radio Norfolk, and not long after getting back I was live on-air chatting to the ever-supportive Stephen Bumfrey.

'So what have been the highlights so far?' he asked.

'Well, playing on some of the small Scottish islands like Colonsay has been incredible,' I replied, 'But also meeting so many people who've helped me along the way.'

Reflecting on the interview afterwards, I realised how lucky I'd been to meet the people I had, and sensed that with much of my journey still to go, it wouldn't be the last time I'd have to rely on the kindness of strangers.

The weather had brightened again by the next morning, and I walked into Staffin to get some supplies. It was Jade's last day on the tour, as the next morning she'd be catching an early bus to Portree, and then a train home. I had to get to Portree later the next day, where I'd be running a songwriting workshop at the Aros Centre and doing a gig in the evening. I was due to be meeting the Russian singer-songwriter from Folkstock Records, Daria Kulesh, and her husband Julian, who'd be joining me on tour for a week. I was especially looking forward to us visiting the Isle of Rum, where my brother, Dave, and family were also coming along to watch us play a gig at the village hall.

Jade and I had one more gig to do that night at the Flodigarry Hotel, which we'd passed on our way from Uig, about six miles north of Staffin. It was a lovely traditional-looking hotel with spectacular views across the Sound of Raasay to the

Scottish mainland. The Dutch owners couldn't have been more welcoming, and we were treated to a gourmet lamb dinner, which the chef had arranged on the plates to look like mini Stone Henges. I was glad that we had such a nice venue to play at for Jade's final night, and we stayed at the bar chatting with the owners and guests until well past midnight.

THIRTEEN

Skye and Rum

I HAD THE hilliest section of Skye to cross the next day, as Bluebell followed the Quiraing for about six miles, coping admirably with everything they threw at her. We were travelling so slowly that I had plenty of time to take in the beauty of the hills, which changed colour constantly as big white clouds billowed by. I reached the top of a huge hill and pulled over to let Bluebell cool down for a while, looking out in awe at the silver sea full of white crested waves, the jagged peaks of the Cuillin mountains looming in the distance.

Skye was voted 'fourth best island in the world' by National Geographic, and I could understand why. It's the second largest island in Scotland, and the biggest of the Inner Hebrides, at 639 square miles. Until the Skye Road Bridge was built in 1995 the only way to get there was by ferry, and today it has a population of around 10,000. The Clearances changed the demographics and culture of the island considerably, with many people forced off their crofts onto transport ships, taking their Gaelic culture with them. There are still 2,000 crofts on Skye, although only about 100 of them are large enough to sustain a full-time living.

The remainder of the journey was mainly downhill, passing Portree's pretty harbour lined with colourful cottages on the way to the Aros Centre. I'd been discussing with Ruiridh, the technical manager of the theatre, the possibility of putting Bluebell onto the stage for the evening performance. It would be the only venue on the tour where I would have the opportunity do this, as the side doors of the theatre led directly onto the stage, which had a sunken auditorium. Ruiridh came out to meet me when I arrived, and we took some measurements to check whether Bluebell could fit through the side doors. It would be a tight squeeze but it did look possible, although there was also a giant totem pole in the courtyard that would have to be moved out of the way first.

Not long after I'd arrived, Daria and Julian turned up. It was really nice to see Daria again, as the last time we'd met had been in a cafe in Knebworth, when doing my tour by milk float had just been the seed of an idea. Daria had first come to Skye as an interpreter for the Moscow State Orchestra, and like many that visit, the place had captured her heart. We spent the rest of the afternoon chatting in the cafe, until Ruiridh came to find us and said he was ready to move Bluebell. Eight of us, including Daria and Julian, heaved the massive totem pole in the courtyard out of the way until there was enough room to get Bluebell past. We then had to clear all manner of obstacles out of the way in the theatre, moving lighting rigging, stage props and cables until there was room to get Bluebell onto the stage. The plan was to reverse on, as there would be no room to turn Bluebell round, and I wanted the hatch facing the audience.

I edged Bluebell back, and there was a loud crack as the rear wheels entered stage left. If we fell through the stage, it would certainly be a dramatic way to end the tour! After a tense minute or two of careful manoeuvring, we finally had Bluebell in position, and she looked amazing. The main theatre spotlights lit her up in a wash of blue and purple, and as a finishing touch Ruiridh put a couple of huge bamboo plants either side. Once we'd done the soundcheck there was barely enough time to get changed before the evening performance started.

Daria was on first, playing a lovely mixture of her own and traditional Russian folk songs. It was great to be on a big stage again, and having Bluebell behind me as I played the songs from my new album spurred me on. After signing CDs afterwards, I loaded my gear back into Bluebell and drove her off stage again. I'd arranged with Ruiridh to sleep in the Aros Centre car park, and our final job was to lead some cables into the theatre so that I could charge Bluebell up for the night. It was pouring down with rain, and we were both wet through by the time we'd finished. I thanked Ruiridh for all his help, and was just settling down for the night when there was a knock on the door. It was Ruiridh again, who said there'd been a power cut. This was bad news as it meant I couldn't get any charge in Bluebell, but there was nothing that could be done until the power company came to have a look in the morning.

Meanwhile a police car turned up, and Ruiridh went over to talk to the officers. I heard something about 'milk float', and 'blown the power', and then the policemen started laughing. I hoped it wasn't me that had caused the power failure, but at least it looked like I wouldn't be spending the night in the local jail. The two policemen gave me a wave as they drove off, and Ruiridh came to check I was ok before leaving. It was an eerie feeling being alone in the pitch dark, although it had been such a long day that it wasn't long before I was sound asleep.

The electricity company arrived the next morning, bringing with them a spare generator. I soon had Bluebell hooked up again, with no sign of the power tripping this time. Luckily, I didn't have to get too much charge in Bluebell anyway, as I was only travelling 20 miles to a campsite near Broadford. I was on the road again by lunchtime, and drove to Sligachan, which marks the beginning of the Cuillin mountains from the northern end of Skye. It was an incredibly beautiful journey with barely a house in sight, just miles of heather, forests and rocky rivers, with small waterfalls coming down the sides of the mountains. The valley coming into Sligachan was spectacular, the imposing Cuillins on either side towering over us as Bluebell plodded her way through. Regarded as being some of the toughest mountains in Scotland to climb, the Cuillins have a distinctive jagged formation, and are a dark black colour due to their formation from basalt. They include 12 Munroes (Scottish mountains over 3,000 feet), which attract walkers from all over the world who pursue the art of 'Munro bagging'.

I settled for a more genteel walk through the heather at Sligachan while Bluebell cooled down, before continuing on the hilliest part of our journey through a mountain pass near a place called Sconser. We came to a set of traffic lights at the bottom of the pass, which had a convoy car leading traffic through. I was near the start of the queue, and when we got past the lights there was soon a massive tailback of cars behind us. The road was narrow and steep, and when I finally pulled over, a long line of cars drove past us hooting as they went.

The mountain had drained Bluebell's batteries, but the remainder of the journey followed the coast road, which was more or less flat to Broadford. I was greeted at my campsite by a spectacular rainbow arching over the tiny island of Scalpay, just across the water. It was a lovely place, a working boat yard that the English owners had bought as part of the business. I spent the rest of the afternoon reading a book and looking out at the boats sailing past, until my brother, Dave, arrived with his family from Aberdeen. My young niece Anna was especially impressed when I gave her a guided tour of Bluebell.

I was glad to see that Anna had brought her favourite teddy bear Polar, who she always took on holiday with her. I took photos every year of Polar, so that I could make a Christmas calendar for Anna about 'Polar's Adventures', which obviously this year would be featuring Bluebell. After driving into Broadford for some fish and chips, we went for a walk along the beach, and then all crammed into Bluebell to drink hot chocolate and watch a film on my tiny TV. We had an early start in the morning, as we needed to get to Armadale by 10am to catch the first of two ferries that would take us to the Isle of Rum. I'd be setting off early with Bluebell to give her time for a rest halfway, and the plan was that Dave would catch up with us, so that Anna could come the remainder of the way in Bluebell. We were also meeting Daria and Julian in Armadale, who'd catch the ferry with Dave and my sister-in-law Anne, and if all went to plan, we'd be on the Isle of Rum in plenty of time for the evening gig.

It was a beautiful journey the next morning, with barely any traffic on the road as I drove along the Sleat Peninsula towards Armadale. After stopping for some breakfast at the top of a hill with views over the Sound of Sleat, I carried on for another few miles until Bluebell was passed by a car with an excited girl clutching a cuddly polar bear, both of them waving madly at me. I pulled over, and Anna climbed aboard for the last few miles to Armadale. We'd be returning there the next day, as I had some gigs lined up through a local music promoter called Duncan MacInnes.

I'd first visited Armadale whilst on holiday two years previously, after seeing a poster advertising a gig featuring Eva Cassidy's brother, Dan. I booked in at a campsite called Rubha Phoil for one night, and was so enchanted by the place, which was tucked away in a bluebell wood next to its own beach, that I stayed five nights. I'd talked to Duncan at the gig, and said how much I'd like to come and play there, never dreaming that I'd return two years later in a milk float! Duncan had booked me to play some gigs for The Skye Festival, including a house concert at Rubha Phoil on the Saturday night.

Daria and Julian were waiting for us when we arrived at the ferry terminal, and we piled everyone's bags and Daria's instruments into the back of Bluebell before Anna and I drove onto the ferry. After parking, we went up to the top deck to meet the others and enjoy the views as we sailed over to the small town of Mallaig, where our next ferry took us to Rum. It was a spectacular crossing, passing the isles of Eigg and Muck, which along with the tiny island of Canna, form the Small Isles.

Rum is the largest of the islands in terms of size, at 41 square miles, but has a population of just 30 people.

All of the islands have a distinctive character and geography of their own, with Rum perhaps being the most dramatic, as it has mountains and a variety of wildlife such as red deer and white-tailed sea eagles. I sensed that life on the island was fairly laid-back as it normally took several weeks to get a reply to my emails. I still didn't know where we were all staying for the night, although Fliss, the lady who'd booked me to play, had assured me that all would be sorted out when we arrived. After pulling into the tiny harbour at Rum, Anna and I drove off the ferry and stopped near a lifeboat hut to wait for the others. There was no sign of Fliss, who I'd thought was going to meet us, but eventually an electric buggy pulled up with a signplate with 'Rum 1' written on it.

A guy with a beard and long hair jumped out and walked over with a big grin, saying, 'I'm Chainsaw Dave. Fliss has gone to Italy for the week, but she asked me to come and meet you.'

'Oh great,' I replied, grateful that at least we were expected. 'Do you know if any accommodation arrangements have been made?'

'Well, I've got a caravan that you can use,' said Chainsaw Dave, 'And I think some of you are booked in at the lodge.'

By this time the rest of the party had arrived, and my brother said that they were booked into camping pods at the lodge. Daria and Julian said they didn't mind sleeping in the caravan, which just left me to be sorted out. 'I'll need to charge Bluebell up overnight,' I told Chainsaw Dave, who said I could park up in the lifeboat hut. It sounded like we had a plan! Chainsaw Dave had bought his 'Rum 1' buggy after the London Olympics, when the vehicles had been sold off cheaply. The buggy had enough room to carry eight passengers and their luggage, and was used for transporting tourists around the island.

There are no paved roads on Rum, and I was in my element as Bluebell followed a forest track that led around the side of the island to the tiny village of Kinloch. We stopped at a large eco-lodge to unload Dave and Anne's things, and carried on through the grounds of Kinloch Castle to the village, which has just a few cottages, a village hall and a tiny post office that doubled up as the island's only shop and pub.

We arranged to meet Daria and Julian later on, and Dave, Anne, Anna and myself went to do some exploring around the island. Archaeological studies have shown that Rum was populated as early as the 8th Century BC, and after passing hands from Vikings to Scottish Lords, it fell to a similar fate as the other islands I'd visited, when between 1826 and 1828 virtually its entire population of 400 was shipped off to Nova Scotia. The feelings of the locals were poignantly expressed by one of the few shepherds allowed to remain, who wrote:

> *'The people of the island were carried off in one mass, forever, from the sea-girt spot where they were born and bred... The wild outcries of the men and heart-breaking wails of the women and children filled all the air between the mountainous shore of the bay.'*

The landowner who'd sent them away bought 8,000 sheep to farm on Rum, but was bankrupt by 1839 due to the price of mutton and wool falling. The island was eventually bought by Sir George Bullough, who built Kinloch Castle and turned Rum into a sporting estate for shooting, which is why there is such a large population of red deer on Rum today. Following Sir George's death, the island was sold in 1957 for £23,000 to Scottish National Heritage, who still own it.

After our walk, I started setting up for the evening gig in the hall and got chatting to some of the locals. I wondered how they kept themselves entertained in the winter, and somebody joked that quite a few people had left in straight-jackets. A good mixture of locals, tourists and geology students had gathered by early evening outside the post office, enjoying a beer or two before the music started. Daria kicked proceedings off, and during the interval I got Anna onto the stage with Polar to sing a song from the musical '*Annie*'. The party carried on well into the night, but I eventually made my excuses and drove back to the lifeboat hut to get Bluebell on charge. I sat up for a while watching the moonlight on the water, falling asleep to the sound of the resident Rum blues band drifting across the ocean.

FOURTEEN

Many Rivers to Cross

I WAS GETTING ready to leave the next morning when I suddenly realised I'd left a bag containing all my microphones and leads at the village hall. The ferry was already pulling in, and Chainsaw Dave had warned me that it wouldn't wait for me if I was late. It would take too long to get to the hall and back in Bluebell, but luckily Chainsaw Dave turned up and asked one of the locals to give me a lift to the hall in a pick-up truck. We sped round the island, passing my brother Dave, Anne and Anna, who'd managed to get lost, and were sprinting for the ferry. Luckily, my bag of leads was in the hall where I'd left it, and I grabbed it and jumped back in the pick-up truck for the return leg.

Chainsaw Dave had managed to sweet-talk the CalMac guys into waiting for us all, and I was told I'd need to reverse onto the ferry so that Bluebell would be facing the right way when we reached Mallaig. It was the steepest ramp I'd had to get up so far, and Bluebell ran out of power about halfway up. A crowd of people were watching from the ferry as I drove back down the ramp to get a longer run-up. This time I reversed so quickly I couldn't see what I was doing in my wing mirrors, and I just hoped that I'd got my line right, otherwise I would have been over the side into the Atlantic Ocean! I received a round of applause from the amused spectators as I finally embarked on the ferry, and breathed a huge sigh of relief.

It was a longer journey this time back to Mallaig, as the ferry was taking a different route, stopping at all of the Small Isles on the way. Much as I wanted to enjoy the scenery, I was feeling tired and dizzy, and tried to get some sleep in the ferry lounge. The only problem with my plan was that Anna had eaten a breakfast of Cocoa Pops and a Mars Bar washed down with hot-chocolate, and had decided to sing her entire repertoire of 'Annie' songs! I eventually gave up on the idea of sleep, and went up to the top deck just as we were passing Canna. It was a remote outpost, with the ruins of a church next to its harbour, and a couple of crofts lining its shores. I felt sad that this would be the last ferry ride of the tour, as it had been such an interesting way of travelling. As we were pulling into Armadale, I phoned Duncan MacInnes to let him know that we would shortly be arriving.

'That's fantastic,' said Duncan, who'd been very supportive of my mad-cap milk float adventure. 'We've got a good crowd waiting for you at the ferry car park.'

Duncan had kindly offered to let myself, Daria and Julian stay at his house for a couple of nights, and Dave, Anne and Anna were booked into a B+B. When we arrived at Armadale, Duncan was waiting for us looking suitably eccentric, wearing a pair of shorts with a jacket, and carrying a huge umbrella with a picture of a strawberry on it. There were posters up at the ferry terminal announcing Bluebell's arrival, and Duncan guided me to a spot on the car park that CalMac had reserved for me. I soon had my music gear set up, performing to a crowd of around 200 people, and was about to play my song 'Holiday' when a Spanish guy came up to me, saying he was on honeymoon and could I dedicate a song to his wife.

It was perfect timing, and everyone gave the newlyweds a big round of applause when I made the dedication over the microphone. After doing a few more songs, Daria and Julian helped me carry all the music gear up to Rhuba Phoil, where we were playing that night. Our gig was in a big workshop that had been transformed into a performance space, crammed full of benches and make-shift seats ready for the evening event. Duncan had been doing a great job of publicising the gig, and I was hopeful that we'd get a good crowd. I left Bluebell in the ferry car park, and drove with Dave to Duncan's house, which was a couple of miles out of Armadale. It was a beautiful old house with a sprawling garden leading down to a private beach. Duncan introduced me to his wife Polly, who'd been busy cooking us a delicious chicken stew, and seemed to take all of the visitors in her stride.

'Oh, Duncan's always inviting people,' Polly modestly told me when I thanked her for her hospitality. 'Last week we had a whole dance troupe here.'

Back at Rhuba Phoil, I attempted to get Bluebell up the steep slope to the workshop, managing to get stuck halfway up. Eventually abandoning her back in the ferry car park, I crept into the workshop and sat with Dave, Anne and Anna while Daria played the opening songs. The place was packed, and I really enjoyed my set, playing some old songs and new, and telling the audience about my journey so far.

The next morning, I went with Duncan to put some posters up advertising the house concert I was doing that evening at Duncan and Polly's, and then we drove to an art gallery about eight miles away, where I'd be returning in the afternoon to do a short concert. When we got back to Duncan's I fetched my map to see if he and Polly had any suggestions about how I could get to Dingwall, near Inverness, where I had some gigs in a week's time. The most direct route was far too hilly, and the longer, flatter route didn't have any campsites that I could stop to charge up on the way. I had to drive to a gig at Kyleakin, just before the Skye bridge, the next day, and Duncan said he knew the owner of a garage just over the bridge at Kyle of Lochalsh, who might be able to transport me fairly cheaply to Dingwall. Meanwhile, Dave, Anne and Anna had called in to say goodbye, and we arranged to meet again in Edinburgh in a couple of weeks. After waving them off, I took Bluebell to Duisdalebeg for my afternoon gig, a lovely old church that had been converted into an art gallery that displayed paintings by local artists.

When I got back, Polly had been busy cooking us all another slap-up meal. We were playing in Duncan's study that night, a big wood-panelled room full of old books, family photos and an antique piano. The room had fantastic acoustics, and after doing a soundcheck we waited for the guests to arrive. Duncan said he thought there would be several families along, and suggested I gave the children a ride in Bluebell during the interval. We had a small but very appreciative audience that night, and I enjoyed hearing about Daria's Russian family history which had inspired her songs. It was nice that Julian always sat near the front listening intently to Daria, even though he must have heard her songs and stories many times before. The children's faces lit up at the interval when I said, 'Right, who wants a go on the back of the milk float!' It was drizzling outside, but under the shelter of Duncan's strawberry umbrella, the children climbed into the back of Bluebell, and with the hatch still open we drove up and down Duncan's driveway, skidding to a halt each time to make the children laugh.

I was feeling dizzy again the next morning and stayed in bed, as I had a late-night gig to do that evening at a backpackers called Saucy Mary's in Kyleakin. Duncan phoned the garage at Kyle of Lochalsh, and arranged for Bluebell to be transported to Dingwall the next day, which would take all the pressure off me over the coming week. Daria and Julian left mid-morning for Kyleakin, and I followed them after lunch, retracing my route through the Sleat Peninsula.

The mountain vistas were incredible, with swathes of purple heather blowing in the wind, and I took my time to appreciate my last day on Skye. I reached Kyleakin by late afternoon, a sweet little village overlooking the Skye Bridge, with just a few hotels, a little shop and a harbour at the end of the road. Jonathan, the owner of Saucy Mary's, was really friendly and said we could order whatever we wanted from the menu.

I was feeling a bit better by the time we started playing, but it was still one of the toughest gigs I'd had to do on the tour so far. All the late nights and travelling had finally caught up with me, and I desperately needed some rest and recuperation. There was a lively backpacker crowd in the bar as I struggled through my set longing for bed. It was well past midnight by the time we finished playing, and I gave Daria and Julian a hug goodbye, as I'd be leaving early in the morning for the Kyle of Lochalsh.

I was treated to a salmon and poached egg breakfast the next morning before setting off in Bluebell for the Skye Bridge. The view was even more beautiful than I'd remembered, passing a lighthouse with boats sailing beneath the bridge, the grandeur of the Scottish mainland mountains rising in the distance. I was soon at the garage in Kyle of Lochalsh, where a huge transporter lorry was waiting to take Bluebell and myself to Dingwall. Neil, my driver, was very friendly, and we chatted all the way about life, the universe and nothing in particular.

I was booked onto a campsite near the Ross County football ground, where I'd camped a few years previously during a tour I did with a disabled musician friend. That had been a big adventure in its own right, as we attempted John O' Groats to Lands End with me cycling, and my friend Tim driving a disability scooter. Unfortunately, the tour had ended at Loch Ness after we burnt the motor out on his scooter, but we'd had a lot of fun along the way, even if we had been a few hundred miles short of our destination!

After settling in at my campsite, I cooked some supper and went for a walk to a little bridge overlooking the Cromarty Firth. It was very peaceful watching the tidal flats with just the sound of wading birds, but I was feeling really homesick. I missed my creature comforts, my friends, and my family. I phoned my dad and gave him an update on my travels, and we talked about how he'd been coping with the cancer. I knew he was finding it tough with me being away for so long, and after we'd finished on the phone I had a long cry, as all the emotion of thinking about my dad and the pressures of the tour came pouring out.

I phoned my promoter friend Rob Ellen the next morning to let him know I'd arrived, and he said he'd be along in an hour or so to show me round Dingwall, and work out a plan of action for the various events he had lined up for me. It was great to finally meet up, and we drove Bluebell into Dingwall with Rob filming the journey. It would be a busy week, as I had an afternoon gig in a couple of days at the Greenhouse, a community centre in Dingwall, and then would be driving to a small town called Strathpeffer, where I was staying at a hotel called The Crystal House, and doing another gig in the evening.

Rob presented a weekly radio show from a studio in Ullapool, a couple of hours drive north of Dingwall, and said he'd lined up an interview with me on his show later in the week, and a support-slot with a Canadian singer-songwriter who was on tour, Kenny Butterill. After that, I had a gig at The Market Bar in Inverness, from where I'd be making my way to Belladrum Festival for a weekend of non-stop music. I spent a lovely afternoon with Rob listening to traditional Scottish music at the Greenhouse, courtesy of some local music students, and then set up outside with Bluebell, playing a few songs on the street to help promote my upcoming gig. Rob said he'd see me the following evening at an open mic event at the Greenhouse, and after finishing my set I drove back to the campsite for a quiet night.

The next morning, I walked back to the Greenhouse for some breakfast, and then went for a look around the town. Dingwall's claim to fame is being the birthplace of King MacBeth, who ruled Scotland from 1040 until 1057, and it once had the largest castle in Scotland north of Sterling. I took Bluebell for a spin into the countryside and ended up by chance at the offices of the Rosshire Journal, who'd done a big feature on my tour a few weeks earlier. I called into the offices and got chatting to Hector, the head reporter who'd written the article, and we went outside to take some photos of us together in front of Bluebell.

There was a really friendly atmosphere at the open mic night, which was full of musicians from Dingwall and surrounding areas. Rob introduced me to some of his friends, including Donald 'Cigarbox' Jack, a great guy who looked like Father Christmas, and built his own guitars out of cigar-boxes. Donald told me how cigar-box guitar making has become a popular art form in recent times, and there is even a yearly convention in France for their makers. He showed me some photos of his guitars, which included one whose neck had been made from gnarled tree roots. I enjoyed listening to the acts playing at the Greenhouse that night, and after I had performed a couple of songs myself, Donald got up and played a song with his cigar-box guitar. Afterwards I walked back to my campsite taking a short-cut along the river. I was grateful to Rob for making me feel so welcome, introducing me to his musical family and making me feel part of their community. I was already feeling much better, and was looking forward to all the events that Rob had lined up for me over the coming week.

FIFTEEN

Belladrum

THERE WAS A good turnout for my gig the following afternoon at The Greenhouse, although a couple of elderly ladies who were sitting in front of me were oblivious to the music, carrying on a loud conversation about various family members' latest news. After playing a couple of songs it became so off-putting that I said to them, 'Excuse me, would you mind sitting at the back if you want to talk.' They looked very offended, and after gulping down their cups of tea disappeared out of the door!

It was great to see Donald there again, who played another couple of songs during the interval on his cigar-box guitar, and after I'd finished the second half of the gig Rob said that he'd treat me to a Thai curry. Rob's partner, Ann, met us at the restaurant, and asked if I'd mind if she came with me in Bluebell to Strathpeffer. It was only about six miles to the Crystal House, and the road was mainly flat, but the driveway up to the entrance was incredibly steep. I did my usual zigzagging routine to the amusement of Rob, who was waiting for us at the top cheering us on.

Rob introduced me to Phil and Serena who ran the Crystal

House, a lovely couple originally from the Midlands who had swapped city life for the slower pace of rural Lanarkshire. Phil showed me up to my room on the third floor, which had a fantastic view over the rooftops of Strathpeffer to the hills in the distance. Kenny Butterill, the Canadian singer-songwriter who I'd be playing a support slot for, was in the room opposite with his band, and we soon got chatting. Although Kenny originated from Canada, he now lived in a cabin in a remote part of California where he ran a recording studio, and had recorded recently with Donovan. He introduced me to his guitarist, Dave, who'd come with him from California, and Gary, a harmonica player from Glasgow who Rob had hooked them up with. They were playing only their third gig together that night, but it sounded like they'd been having a lot of fun already, with Gary learning Kenny's songs as they went along.

The gig was downstairs in the main dining room, and had a nice intimate atmosphere with candles on the tables and huge velvet curtains draped behind the band. After playing an opening set, I enjoyed listening to Kenny's music, which had a laid-back country-blues feel, and Dave and Gary were both sensitive musicians who knew how to add just the right amounts of guitar and harmonica to back up Kenny's guitar playing and singing. I joined the guys in the bar afterwards and had them in tears with laughter as I told them about some of the adventures on my tour. It took a while for Kenny and Dave to get their heads around the concept of a milk float, as they don't have anything similar in America, but once they'd grasped it, they embraced the Milk Float Dimension with huge enthusiasm.

'You should come and do a tour over in the States,' suggested Kenny, although I wasn't sure how well Bluebell would cope with crossing the Sierra Nevada to get to Kenny's neck of the woods!

I had to be up early the next morning to meet Rob, who was driving over with his campervan to take it for its annual MOT, and then he wanted a hand afterwards taking some equipment to Belladrum. We had to do a hill start to get Rob's battered old campervan going again, and I followed him in Bluebell back to Dingwall. If the police had been around, I'm sure between us we would have accumulated a novel's worth of traffic offences! Rob said that I could park up at his house for the next couple of days, and after dropping Bluebell off I drove Rob's car to Belladrum, following his campervan which he wanted to leave on site for the weekend.

'What happened to the MOT?' I asked Rob when we got there.

'Och, it's too much hassle,' he replied. 'I'll sort it out when the festival's over, or I might just leave the damn thing where it is until next year!'

On the way back to Dingwall we stopped off to see a friend of Rob's, a guy called Bertie who ran a 2CV hire company. Rob had been hoping to get me the use of a 2CV for a couple of days so that I could park Bluebell at Belladrum, and have some transport to get to my gig at Inverness. Unfortunately, the only 2CV Bertie had in stock was in need of some maintenance, although Bertie kindly offered to let me park Bluebell at his house for a night on my way to Belladrum. Rob said he could give me a lift into Inverness to do my gig and drop me back at Bertie's, which was only a few miles from Belladrum, so it sounded like we had a plan. We drove back to Dingwall for a quick snack at Rob's, and then went to the Cromarty Firth to collect some beers that the Cromarty Brewing Company were donating for the performers on Rob's stage at Belladrum.

Cromarty is at the end of the Black Isle, a peninsula in between Dingwall and Inverness, and a place I've always been fascinated by after hearing its name on the BBC Shipping News. We followed a single-track road with redundant oil rigs standing like leggy monsters in the firth, passing the beautifully named village of Jemimaville on the way to Cromarty, which is at the end of the peninsula. The Cromarty Brewing Company was down a track just out of the village, and after loading up a trailer with beers we stopped in Cromarty for an ice cream, eating them as we looked out at the oil rigs and boats coming and going in the Firth. Afterwards we drove back to Dingwall, where Ann had prepared a huge roast meal for us. Rob had to go out again that evening to do the sound at a gig for Kenny Butterill, and I took the opportunity to catch up on some emails and get an early night, sleeping soundly in the back of Bluebell, who was parked out on the street.

I had an emotional telephone call with my dad the next morning as it was his birthday, and he was going to hospital the following day for his operation. To help take my mind off things, I spent the rest of the morning doing some planning for my journey from Belladrum to Edinburgh. There was no easy way to get there, as whichever way I went would involve crossing some big mountain ranges. After going through the possible routes on my gradient website, it looked like the best option would be to drive from Belladrum along the shores of Loch Ness, and then past Ben Nevis and across Glen Coe to Perth, where a friend of Rob's had offered to put me up for a couple of nights. From Perth, it would only take two days to reach Edinburgh.

Later that afternoon I drove with Rob and Ann up to Ullapool, which was officially the most northerly point I'd been on my tour. Much as I'd have liked to have taken Bluebell, it was a hilly 60-mile journey with barely a house in sight, and would have taken me four days to get there and back! After looking round the pretty harbour, we stopped at the Argyll Hotel to set up for the evening gig. Kenny Butterill and the boys were already there, and I drove with them to the Lochbroom FM studio on the edge of town, where Rob was preparing for his radio show. I've been in some nice green rooms in my time, but I have to say the guest area at Lochbroom FM is the most beautiful I've ever seen. Its huge windows look directly onto a mountain range whose colours changed dramatically as the clouds swept over their summit, and I had a peaceful half hour sitting drinking tea and gazing out while Kenny and his band did the first part of the show. I was nice and relaxed by the time Rob called me into the studio and started my interview.

'Welcome Paul. It's been the best of times, it's been the worst of times I think could be the best way to describe your tour by milk float so far…'

'There have definitely been a lot of ups and downs!' I replied.

'And you can't really do those in a milk float can you?' said Rob.

'Well...no. My milk float Bluebell's not keen on steep hills, and we've had one or two breakdowns – mechanical not emotional I may add!'

The interview continued like this with Rob and me bantering away, and I played a couple of songs from my new album. Afterwards we went back to the Argyll Hotel, where we had a meal before I did an opening set in the bar. Kenny told me that they'd added an impromptu rhythm section the previous night, asking a member of the audience to play a shaker that Kenny had made from a water bottle and some lentils.

'So what's your lentil-shaking like?' Kenny asked me.

'Uhh...not so bad,' I replied, 'Although I haven't had the chance to practise too much recently.'

'Ok, you're in.' said Kenny, handing me the lentil-shaker. 'Me and Dave like to keep half a pace behind the beat. Just keep things nice and loose and you'll be fine.'

I wasn't really sure what Kenny meant, so just sat in the corner shaking my lentils and hoping for the best. It seemed to work, as at the end of the night I got a massive round of applause when Kenny introduced the different band members. I wondered if maybe I'd missed my vocation, as this was the warmest reception I'd had in a long while, and I made a mental note to add a lentil-shaker to my live show!

I slept in until late the following morning, before packing up ready for the next leg of my journey. The plan was to drive to Bertie's at Kirkhill, which was about 14 miles away, where Rob would meet us before going to Belladrum to do some organising. I then had to get back to Bertie's to pick up my music gear, and Rob would take me to my gig at The Market

Bar in Inverness. I thanked Ann for all her hospitality, and she said that she'd see me at Belladrum. The road to Kirkhill was flat most of the way, passing through the town of Beauly, where I'd stopped for a night with my friend Tim on our way to Loch Ness. It was strange seeing the campsite at Beauly that we'd stayed at 10 years previously, which looked exactly the same, with a large wooden recreation room near its entrance that Tim and I had performed in. Despite having MS, Tim was a talented guitarist who'd played with some of the biggest names in the business, and we'd taken several instruments with us on the trip, including a guitar, mandolin and bagpipes. We had a little trailer built for all the equipment, but unfortunately the weight proved too much and burnt the motor out on the scooter.

We managed to get a repair done on the motor at Beauly, and continued to Drumnadrochit on the shores of Loch Ness, where the axle on the trailer broke. The motor had started playing up again, and we decided to call it a day on the trip, which should have taken us all the way to Lands End. We ended up camping at Drumnadrochit for almost a week while we waited for a friend to come and collect us in his van. My route after Belladrum would take me directly past the campsite at Drumnadrochit, and I was determined that this time I'd make it to my destination, feeling in some way that I was completing my journey for both of us.

From Beauly, I turned up a steep road that led past some woods towards Kirkhill, and was soon at Bertie's. Rob arrived not long afterwards, and during several cups of tea we discussed how we were going to get Bertie's broken 2CV to Belladrum, which would be on display next to Rob's stage. It was a fantastic looking car, with musical notes covering the black and white bodywork, and Rob told me that he'd done a tour in it a few years ago with an American singer-songwriter.

Bertie said he'd got a trailer that we could use to transport the 2CV, but it was a very tight fit, and when Bertie tried to drive up the ramps onto the trailer he got his line wrong, and the wing of the car got stuck on the side of the trailer. To make matters worse one of the ramps fell off, and Rob and I had to heave the car up while Bertie put the ramp back in place. Needless to say, the language was becoming quite colourful as Rob and Bertie argued about whose fault it was that the operation had gone wrong, and ever the diplomat I offered to steer the 2CV to Belladrum if Rob wanted to tow it instead. Bertie couldn't drive as he'd lost his licence, and they both agreed that towing it would be the best way to go.

We reversed the 2CV back down from the trailer and hooked a rope up to Rob's car, but unfortunately Rob forgot to attach it to the 2CV and drove halfway down the road before realising that I was still stationary! When we finally got on the road to Belladrum Rob was only doing about 40mph, but I felt absolutely terrified behind the wheel as I had no control over the steering, and was travelling much faster than I'd become used to in the Milk Float Dimension. As we bumped and jolted along I genuinely feared for my life, and breathed a huge sigh of relief when we turned off the main road onto a county lane that led to Belladrum.

It was late afternoon by the time we got back to Bertie's, and I phoned my brother to see how things had gone with my dad's operation. It was great news – everything had gone well and my dad was expected to return home the next day. It was such a relief knowing that he was ok, and I could now fully concentrate on getting the tour completed. Bertie cooked me some tea to fuel me for the evening gig, and Rob turned up again early evening to take me to Inverness.

I was looking forward to playing the Market Bar, which had a long musical history, and was the place where the Proclaimers were first discovered. After setting up my music gear on the tiny upstairs stage, I went for a look round Inverness. The last time I'd been here was as a six year-old on a family holiday, and I could remember watching a military bagpipe band marching through the town centre. Inverness is a beautiful city, with a river running through the centre, and is the main music hub of the Highlands, with music happening every night of the week all over town.

The Market Bar liked to keep live music going until about 12.30pm to attract late night drinkers, so I had to pace the night carefully to make sure I had enough material. I played a few instrumentals and covers in the first half of the evening, and performed the songs from my new album in the second half. They were an appreciative audience, but it had been a long day and I was glad when Rob and Bertie turned up at the end to give me a hand getting my gear back down the narrow stairs to Rob's car. It was 2am by the time I got to bed, and I had a big day ahead as I needed to get to Belladrum early in the morning to avoid all the queues of festival goers.

I woke the next morning feeling fresh as a daisy, and was soon on the road again. It was only four miles to Belladrum, which is the name of the huge farm that the festival is held at. I was just turning up the track towards the farm when Rob came up behind me in his car – perfect timing! We had to queue for an hour or so while we waited for stewards to guide us onto site, and I was directed to the Hothouse Field, which didn't look an ideal location for Bluebell, as I had a big roller-disco next to me, as well as a rave tent in the adjoining field. The music wasn't due to start until the following day, and I wanted to get one of Rob's awnings up before then, so that if it rained the performers would have some shelter.

When Rob turned up with the awning, we spent almost an hour trying to figure out how the frame fitted together, until we realised there was a corner piece missing. We bodged it together with some masking tape, but the whole thing was lopsided and the flaps were falling down all over the place. I spent another hour tightening it up with guide ropes and taping the flaps back, until in the end it looked really good. There wasn't much else I needed to do for the rest of the day, so I helped Rob over at The Potting Shed Stage, and had a go on Bertie's electric bike that he'd turned up on. Bertie had bought the bike after losing his driving licence, and was hoping to get fit into the bargain, although I wasn't sure he was going about things the right way. Not long after arriving, he said he felt sick from cycling so quickly, and disappeared to the portaloos.

'I'll be alright after I've had a smoke,' he said on his return.

I spent the evening checking out the different acts, including The Proclaimers who were headlining. After a few late nights in a row I was ready for bed, but it took me almost two hours to get to sleep as the deep bass coming from the rave tent was causing Bluebell to shake, rattle and roll.

Bertie re-appeared the next morning looking as if he'd been dragged through a hedge backwards.

'Did you have a good night, Bertie?' I enquired.

'Yeah, I got absolutely hammered and crashed out in Rob's awning,' replied Bertie cheerfully.

I made him some breakfast, and he said he'd see me later as he wanted to go home on his bike and freshen up before the rest of the day's proceedings. I spent the morning putting posters up advertising the acts who were playing on the Milk Float Stage that day, and got set up ready for the first act to arrive. The music was due to start at midday and continue until 9pm, but it soon became apparent that I was going to have to compete to be heard above the noise of the roller-disco, which was already pumping out annoying chart music.

I had some fantastic acts playing, and I did my best to encourage the audience to come in closer so that they could appreciate the music. Rob and Donald played together in a band called The Slim Panatellas who stole the day, with Donald playing his cigar-box guitar, Rob plucking a one-stringed bass instrument, and various other artists joining them on stage, including Rob's brother Mark on drums, who'd played for several years with the prog-rock band Vanity Fayre.

Rob's friend Mairi turned up in the afternoon, who I was due to be staying with in Perth. It was great to meet her as she'd been so encouraging of the tour, helping Rob with publicity for the gigs I'd been doing in Scotland. Mairi's son, Mikey, was due to be playing the Milk Float Stage with his band The Carloways, but by the time he arrived the noise coming from the roller-disco was even louder than it had been earlier. Mikey's band members refused to play, and I can't say I blamed them, as it had got to the point where we couldn't hear ourselves anymore.

I had a really good singer-songwriter from America called Charlie Roth performing before I was due to start, but after playing two songs, he said, 'I'm sorry, I just can't carry on. This is the worst gig of my life.' I felt absolutely terrible, but there was nothing more I could do, as I'd already complained to the organisers, who'd said they couldn't move me until the following day because of site restrictions. Luckily Rob stepped in, and said, 'Ok, let's call it a night. You can all come over and play at The Potting Shed Stage.'

Bertie miraculously appeared again the next morning, having spent another night in Rob's awning. I'd run out of milk as usual, so we went to a cafe for some breakfast, and then I waited around for one of the organisers to come and move me. My main concern was transporting the awning which had taken so long to put together, but a really nice steward helped pack it down with me and put it up again on the field that I was eventually moved to. It was a much better location in a walled garden, with no loud music to contend with, and lots of stalls and marquees doing interesting things like musical instrument making. The first band playing the Milk Float Stage turned up at midday, and we soon had a good crowd gathered round. I asked one of the acts, Dave Rudge, to run the stage for me while I went over to play another set on Rob's stage, and had a great time playing the songs from my new album to the biggest audience of my tour so far.

I got back to Bluebell just as it started pouring down with rain, and we had a real job squeezing the acts into the awning with the speakers and all their equipment. I sat in the back of Bluebell drinking tea and enjoying the music, and was glad that Charlie Roth was booked to play again so that I could make up for the chaos of the previous day. It stopped raining by the time Charlie turned up early evening with another guitarist, Matt Morrow. Matt was a fantastic local musician that Charlie played with whenever he toured Scotland, and they worked really well together, with Matt playing lead guitar to complement Charlie's beautiful tunes.

By the time Charlie and Matt finished playing it was getting late, and after packing away I went over to the Potting Shed Stage to say goodbye to Rob, as I'd be leaving early the next morning. Rob had been getting into the festival spirit and was dancing away to his niece's band, who were headlining the Potting Shed Stage. We gave each other a big hug, and Rob said 'Haste ye back' when I told him how much I'd loved my time up in the Highlands.

SIXTEEN

Ben Nevis and Beyond

Sure enough Bertie turned up again the next morning, and we had some breakfast together before taking the awning down and dropping it off at the Potting Shed Stage. There was no sign of Rob, who was undoubtedly fast asleep in his campervan. I had a big queue of festival traffic behind me as I turned onto the main road to Drumnadrochit, and spotted a police-check ahead. I pulled over to let the queue of traffic behind me get past, taking the opportunity to put my seat-belt on for the first time since leaving Norfolk. I thought for sure the police would stop me, but as I approached they watched me with surprise and then obvious amusement as they waved me through.

There were some steep climbs on the road ahead, and the longest downhill of my tour so far led into Drumnadrochit, at the northern end of Loch Ness. The hill was so steep that I had my foot jammed on the brake the whole way down, and there was a horrible smell of burning by the time we reached the bottom. I stopped in Drumnadrochit to let Bluebell cool down, and took the opportunity to buy some postcards. I had one friend who still didn't believe I'd left Norfolk, and he wanted me to send a postcard from Loch Ness to prove I'd actually been there! I was glad to leave Drumnadrochit, though, as I'd been superstitiously worrying that history would repeat itself, and that I was going to break down and have to call an end to the tour. As I drove out of the town, I thought of my friend Tim, and gave Bluebell a big pat on the steering wheel to celebrate us getting further than last time!

Loch Ness was beautiful, but I had huge queues of impatient holidaymakers behind me for most of the way, as there were hardly any passing places that I could pull into. I'd had virtually no complaints from drivers since I'd left Norfolk, but suddenly I found myself surrounded by angry drivers taking dangerous risks to overtake. I was travelling 30 miles that day to Fort Augustus at the southern end of Loch Ness, and the hills were really draining the batteries. The meter was flashing red for the last five miles, and I was more glad to see my campsite than any other on my tour so far.

I had a quiet night cooking a meal in the back of Bluebell, taking a walk along the shores of Loch Ness afterwards. A stone tower marked the beginning of the loch, which looked really pretty with fishing boats moored at its edge and mountains either side forming a big V on the horizon. It was just what I needed to relieve the stress of driving, and after spending some time catching up on tour emails I got to bed early with a book.

I was on the road by mid-morning the next day, and had a long journey ahead to Fort William, where I was staying on a campsite at the foot of Ben Nevis. The day after would be my birthday, and I was planning to take the day off to climb Britain's highest mountain. I had another long line of drivers tooting away as they overtook me on the way to Fort William. It was an incredibly spectacular road, though, with a high-ridged valley on one side, forests and rivers on the other, and a smattering of lovely old Scottish hotels. I stopped after about 20 miles at the small town of Spean Bridge, parking in the grounds of a watermill that had been turned into a tourist attraction. After eating a sandwich, I had a nap in the back of Bluebell, drifting off to the sound of the river below, and when I woke a big motorhome had pulled into the space next to me. I'd left Bluebell's hatch open as it was a warm day, and the driver of the motorhome was peering inquisitively into the back.

'Sorry to disturb you,' he said, 'but I think your vehicle's absolutely amazing.'

After all the irate drivers I'd been dealing with, I was grateful to see a friendly face. The man invited his brother and elderly mother to come and look round, and the mother was especially enthusiastic.

'I think you're really brave travelling all this distance in a milk float,' she said.

The brothers told me they were on their way from Glasgow to the Outer Hebrides to do some fishing, and I thought it was lovely that they'd brought their mother along. I gave them a copy of my CD to enjoy on the way, and set off for Fort William refreshed in the knowledge that there were some friendly holidaymakers in the area after all. It wasn't long before the majesty of Ben Nevis came into view, which despite being midsummer, still had snow on its summit. By the time I reached my campsite it had started raining, and I watched a line of tired and wet walkers returning from the mountain. I hoped the rain would clear the following day for my climb, although whatever the weather I was really proud that Bluebell and I had made it to Britain's highest peak.

I woke the next morning with a birthday message on my phone from my dad and brother Andy singing Happy Birthday. It was the best present I could have wished for, knowing that my dad was safe and well at home again. Ben Nevis was steeped in mist, and I took my time getting my things together for the walk to the top, hoping that the weather would clear by later on. I bought a huge piece of sponge cake from the campsite shop to eat at the top, and made myself a packed lunch, setting off mid-morning just as the drizzle stopped. I walked about a mile from the campsite to a car park, where a footpath followed the river and then forked off onto the trail up to Ben Nevis. The first recorded ascent of Ben Nevis took place in 1771, and in 1818 the poet John Keats climbed to the top, comparing it to 'Mounting ten St Paul's without the convenience of a staircase!' The path that is in use today was built in 1883 for ponies to carry supplies to an observatory, the remains of which can still be seen at the summit.

The first section of the path rose gradually, and I stopped every now and then to look back, as the campsite became a tiny speck in the distance. The next section turned steeper, with steps made from small boulders that I walked up for about an hour. I was already tired and hungry, and stopped to tuck into my sandwiches, watching the walkers go by. The view was spectacular, and made all the effort worthwhile. I could see the whole of Loch Ness, as well as lots of smaller lochs tucked away in between the mountains, that rose as far as the eye could see.

I walked for another 30 minutes until I came to a waterfall at a place called the Red Burn, which had a fast-flowing river that needed to be carefully crossed, and afterwards got chatting to a couple from Yorkshire. The conversation with Lisa and Bill helped to take my mind off my aching limbs, as we approached the final section of the climb, known as the zigzags. It's not until you're about three quarters of the way up the mountain that you can see the summit of Ben Nevis, 4,409 feet above sea level, and we kept wondering how much further we needed to go until we reached the top. It was another world up there, with thick ice and snow in the crevices, and the weather took a turn for the worse when a thick mist descended for our final climb to the top.

Although I didn't have the spectacular views I'd hoped for at the summit, I felt a real sense of achievement, and that somehow the climb was symbolic of my journey. Despite the ups and downs of the tour, I'd made it through, and although we still had a long way to go, I was sure that Bluebell and I were going to make it. After sharing my sponge cake with Lisa and Bill, we started the long walk back down the mountain. There was a nice etiquette on the path where you could talk to people for a while and then drift off at your own pace without the need to explain or say goodbye, perhaps catching up with them again later. I chatted to a man from Taunton who'd survived cancer, and I kept seeing a couple from Birmingham, and we'd say things to each other like, 'It's hot now isn't it?', or maybe half an hour later, 'It's a bit colder now isn't it!' So British!

I was soon back down the mountain, and walked the painful mile back to the campsite. After a well needed shower, I treated myself to some fish and chips, and had more phone calls from friends wishing me happy birthday. I had an early start the next morning as I wanted to get over Glen Coe before any holiday traffic was around, and was planning on leaving the campsite by 6am. My final bit of climbing that day was into my sleeping bag, where I reached the summit of Mount Deep Sleep in a matter of minutes, and stayed there for the rest of the night.

I felt surprisingly fresh when my alarm went off at 5.30am the next morning, and after a quick cup of tea I was on the road, driving along the beautiful A82 that follows the shores of Loch Eil. Apart from the occasional lorry the road was empty, and it was a fantastic feeling being able to appreciate the journey without worrying about holiday traffic. I passed an early morning ferry at Corran chugging across the loch, and turned inland towards Glen Coe, which was still wrapped in mist.

I wanted to give Bluebell a chance to cool down before the long ascent up the Glen, and pulled over in a lay-by for half an hour before carrying on. It was still another 15 miles to my campsite at Glen Coe Mountain Resort, and as we continued I felt a twinge of anxiety, hoping that Bluebell would be able to make it. The road rose gradually higher, with wide moors appearing either side as the mountains loomed larger. There was still barely any traffic about, and eventually we reached the top of the Glen where the road flattened out onto a plateau.

I'd had to work out my route really carefully as there were no houses for a long way after Glen Coe village, and my campsite was the only place that I could get Bluebell charged up before the next town, 30 miles away. I arrived at Glen Coe Mountain Resort just in time for the cafe opening, where I had a bacon roll and a hot-chocolate to celebrate. The cafe was at the bottom of a ski-lift, and although it was still in use at this time of the year, it was during the winter that the place would fill up with skiers.

There was a huge car park in front of the café with a line of camping pods and a few hard-standing sites for campervans, where I parked Bluebell after breakfast. I spent the rest of the morning in the cafe admiring the view, and doing some tour planning. I'd originally intended to transport Bluebell on a lorry from Edinburgh to Norfolk at the end of the tour, although at the back of my mind was the thought of a possible Guinness World Record. I wanted to rack up as many miles as I could, but the decision would partly depend on whether I had enough money to drive back, as it would add an extra two weeks onto the trip. After a long walk in the afternoon, I cooked a stir-fry and sat with my book watching the mountains as the sun set. The camp site was fairly quiet with only a few walkers staying, and I gave one couple a fright when I banged the window to try and kill some midges, shouting, 'Sod off you little buggers!' I think the couple thought I was shouting at them, and looked quite offended as they hurried back to their tent!

I don't know if it was the mountain air, but I woke up the next morning feeling high as a kite. After a leisurely breakfast, I set off in Bluebell about mid-morning on the road across Ranoch Moor, singing at the top of my voice. There was a lovely hazy light and the moors were in full bloom, covered in long grasses, summer flowers and heather. Ranoch Moor is on a high plateau surrounded by huge snow-capped mountains, and I felt as if I was in Tibet not Scotland. The road gradually descended into a valley full of lochs, rising again to the tiny town of Tyndrum, where I stopped to let Bluebell cool down for a while.

It was an archetypal highland scene, with mountain vistas and a wide, fast-flowing river with two men in waders fly-fishing near a stone bridge. I was travelling about 20 miles that day to a place called Strathfillan Wigwams, where I was booked to play an informal gig. It was a fantastic campsite with wooden camping pods set in a forest near a waterfall. I'd booked the gig at the last minute, and Rena the campsite owner was really friendly, giving me a big wave as I pulled up outside the farm shop at the campsite entrance.

'We've been really looking forward to you coming, and have put posters up so everyone knows about the gig,' she told me.

Rena showed me to my camping pod, which had lovely views of the mountains from its porch. There was a grassy area opposite where I parked Bluebell ready for the gig later on, and after getting her on charge I went for a walk up to the waterfall. The campsite was a maze of camping pods and wooden lodges tucked into their own little spaces amongst the forest, with families sitting outside enjoying some al fresco cooking. After cooking supper myself, I set up for the evening gig and soon had a good crowd.

Rena and all the staff came along to watch, and went

around with a bucket at the end of the evening, collecting almost £200 for me. I was just settling into my camping pod for the night, when a couple of German guys knocked on my door, and asked if they could borrow my guitar. I was very reluctant, as my guitar is something very personal and precious to me, but I said I'd come and play them a couple of songs. I did my version of Don McLean's 'Starry Nights', and got a big round of applause from their children before I finally called it a night.

It was another sunny morning when I got on the road towards Comrie the next day. I was hoping it would be the last really hilly section of my tour before Edinburgh, although as I was to find out I was being a little over-optimistic! My steepest hill that day was at Lochearnhead, which seemed to go on forever, as the road rose through a dense pine forest to the top of a mountain range that looked down on Loch Earn. I was about three quarters of the way up with a big queue behind me when I started to smell burning, and had to quickly pull over.

I was worried that the hill-start would be too much for Bluebell when we got going again, but ever the trooper she just managed to pick up enough speed to get to the top of the hill. From there it was all downhill to Loch Earn, with the road following its pretty shores to Comrie. The entrance to my campsite had a really steep slope, and I had to use all my zigzagging skills to get to the top. The owner had been watching me from his office, and gave me a puzzled look when I called in to see him. I wondered if he thought I'd been drinking, and when I explained about the milk float tour, I think his suspicions were confirmed!

SEVENTEEN

Floating to the Fringe

I SET OFF early the next morning for Perth, stopping at the pretty tourist town of Crieff to buy a present for Mairi, who was putting me up for the night. By total coincidence I parked outside a flower shop called 'Bluebell's Florist'. It was obviously meant to be, as I bought an unusual orange coloured plant, and when I arrived later at Mairi's spotted two orange lamp shades in her living-room, which Mairi said were her favourite colour. The Milk Float Dimension does indeed move in mysterious ways! After looking round Crieff, I asked some directions from an elderly man who was standing admiring Bluebell, and set off on a country road that took me to the small town of Auchterarder. It was a lovely drive through the gentle Perthshire hills, passing tractors harvesting wheat fields, and barely any other traffic in sight.

Mairi lived just outside Perth at a place called Bridge of Earn, and my cross-country route took me more or less to her doorstep. I hadn't realised until I met Mairi at Belladrum that she had cerebral palsy. I'd worked in my care job with several people who suffered from the condition, so I knew how debilitating it could be, but thankfully Mairi was able to live a relatively independent life without the need for a full-time carer. Mairi's son Mikey turned up with his girlfriend Hannah not long after I'd arrived, and we went for a drive in Mairi's specially adapted vehicle. It was an amazing van that loaded Mairi's wheelchair in mechanically, and could be driven with a small steering-wheel that had buttons on that could be used to brake and accelerate.

It was still quite scary doing 70mph on a stretch of dual carriageway on the way into Perth, although I hasten to add that was due to me being used to travelling in the Milk Float Dimension, and nothing to do with Mairi's driving! I was given a guided tour of Perth, which feels like a large town, but has city status due to its cathedral and university. It's a beautiful place, full of old stone buildings, churches and museums. After a coffee in the town centre, Mairi drove me back on the scenic route to Bridge of Earn, following the banks of the Firth of Tay. Mikey had been called off to do a birthday gig for the Gran of the bass player in their band (it's all in a day's work for a musician!), and I treated Mairi to a Chinese meal to say thanks for letting me stay.

I'd promised Mikey and Hannah a ride in Bluebell before I left, so the next morning they climbed into the back as I waved goodbye to Mairi. I dropped Mikey and Hannah off at the local Co-op, and after stocking up on supplies for the next couple of days, I set off for my campsite at Kinross, about 16 miles away. After driving towards Forgandenny, which I'd passed a couple of days previously, I turned off into some beautiful hilly countryside that crossed miles of forest bordered by stone walls. There were no cars around, which was just as well, as I climbed probably the steepest hills of my tour so far, and I had to stop at the top of each valley to let Bluebell cool down.

Apart from the occasional farm there were no houses, and the hills were becoming so steep that I was genuinely starting to panic. I was so close to my goal of reaching Edinburgh, but one wrong turn could easily have put an end to the tour if the motor burnt out again. Eventually I came to a crossroads signposted for Milnathort, which wasn't far from my campsite at Kinross. Bluebell's battery meter was flashing red as I drove the last few miles, but the road flattened out by the time we reached the shores of Loch Leven near to Kinross. I breathed a big sigh of relief when I reached my campsite, and celebrated with a sandwich and afternoon nap. It felt strange being so close to Edinburgh after all the anticipation of the last few months, and I couldn't believe that by the next day I would reach my destination.

I was raring to go as I set off on the road to Edinburgh in the morning, finally floating to the Fringe. My route followed quiet B-roads to Cowdenbeathall, and then Inverkeithing, just before the Forth Bridge, where I pulled over after spotting a sign for a musical instrument repair shop. I'd been having trouble with the pick-up on one of my guitars which had been cutting out during performances, and I called into the shop to see if it was something they could fix. It turned out to be a bagpipe workshop, and I spoke to a friendly Polish guy who showed me a huge lathe he was using to make chanters (the piece you hold to play the notes on bagpipes). I was fascinated to learn how the instruments were made, which was much more technical than you might have expected. The lathe was the size of a small car, and had digital displays that were complicated to navigate, but made the process of making the chanters much faster and more accurate.

My Polish friend gave me the number of somebody in Edinburgh who he thought could fix my guitar, and wished me luck for the Fringe. I was soon on the approach road to the Forth Bridge, surrounded by fast-moving traffic. Much as I wanted to enjoy the moment of crossing into Edinburgh, I had to use all my concentration to watch the road as I turned onto the dual carriageway that led over the bridge. The skyline of Edinburgh jolted up and down in front of me as Bluebell bumped past the joining sections of the bridge, and we eventually turned off onto a B-road that led to the A8. It wasn't long before I spotted some flags with pictures of giant Ninja Turtles on, directing me to the entrance of my campsite at the Royal Highland Centre. The 'Ninja' campsite was a special pop-up campsite that appeared at festival times, with a designated camping area for performers. As I turned off the dual carriageway and drove underneath an archway onto the site, Geoff and Rhyanne the organisers were standing at the entrance waving at me.

'I can't believe you've made it all the way in a milk float!' said Rhyanne, as I gave her the guided tour of Bluebell.

Geoff helped me rig up some extension leads so that I could charge Bluebell from my camping pitch, which was on a small slope not far from the campsite entrance. Rhyanne told me there were 30 performers arriving over the next few days who'd be camping next to me, and Geoff cordoned off my pitch with some bunting so that I'd have room to park each day. I felt immediately at home on the campsite, which was fairly small and had a lovely lake at the centre with water lilies growing on it. Edinburgh airport was close by, but Rhyanne said that after a day or two you got used to the sound of the planes taking off, which you could see rising above the tree-line.

I spent the rest of the day getting settled in, and phoned up Brian at Essential Edinburgh, who'd booked me to play at the Fringe. We arranged to meet the next day on George Street to have a look at the options for spaces where I could perform, and he said that he'd organise a parking permit for me so that I wouldn't have problems with getting moved on by the police. My first performance was in a couple of days, which would give me time to find my way around before the acts that were playing the Milk Float Stage arrived.

I had a full timetable worked out for the next two weeks, with vatious acts playing every day, and it had been quite complicated co-ordinating it so that everybody could come. SamH, who'd played at Barnard Castle, was arriving with his band the following night, and I had a duo called Ethemia playing, who were travelling all the way from Gloucestershire. An Edinburgh based singer-songwriter called Carrie MacDonald was playing after that, as well as Mairi's son Mikey. Steve Young, who'd played earlier in the tour, was also coming, as well as a singer-songwriter from Norfolk called Johnny Steinberg, and Daria Kulesh was playing the final five days up until the end of the Fringe. It would be fantastic to have the company of other musicians while I was in Edinburgh, and I was looking forward to catching up with the friends I'd made earlier in the tour.

It was lovely and hot when I woke the next morning, and I sat outside Bluebell enjoying the sun. I got chatting to a young American woman called Gabrielle, a performance artist who'd recently graduated from drama school and was touring the world. I asked Gabrielle how she'd been finding the Fringe so far, and she told me the first few days had been really tough, and that she'd been virtually ignored until she adapted her show to make it more involving for the audience.

'Yeah, so I'm now called Madame Fish Head,' explained Gabrielle, as she produced a huge mask of a cod head from a bin liner. 'What I do is stand with an ironing board, and grab an item of clothing off a passer-by on the street, and offer to give them a psychic reading for a quid while I iron their clothing.'

I admired Gabrielle for her ingenuity in improvising her new show. She'd left the US with just $2,000 to travel the world for a year, and was making her tour up as she went along. I offered Gabrielle a lift into town, and she piled her various stage props into the back of Bluebell before we set off. Our route took us round the back of the campsite, past the airport, and onto the busy A8. Gabrielle had been into town a few times on the bus, so knew roughly where we needed to go, but I was finding the city traffic very unnerving. The road forked off on a steep hill that had been funnelled with traffic cones into single-lanes, and I had a massive queue of cars behind me by the time we reached the top of the hill. I couldn't figure out whether or not I was allowed to drive in the bus lanes, which cars were using to overtake me on the inside.

When I did finally start driving on the bus lane, the bus drivers started flashing me, so I pulled back onto the outside lane and soon had another queue of cars behind me.

By some small miracle we managed to find our way onto the right part of George Street, and parked a few doors down from the Essential Edinburgh offices. George Street looked an ideal place to perform as most of it was pedestrianised, and after calling in at the Essential Edinburgh offices, Brian showed me the different locations that he said I could park with Bluebell. There was an outdoor market for the next few days on Castle Street, just off George Street, and Brian introduced me to the organiser, Tanya, who was very friendly and said she'd love it if I played there. It was a great spot with a view of the castle, and there were cafes opposite the market where people could sit and listen to the music. Brian said he'd arrange an extra permit so that I could park on Castle Street, and I agreed to play there for the next couple of days.

After my meeting with Brian I drove back to the campsite, as I had Sam and his band arriving early evening, and wanted to be there for them. I managed to get lost in the city centre again, before eventually finding my way to Haymarket Station, which marked the start of the A8. It was slightly less petrifying driving back, and I finally figured out the bus lane system, which was open to all vehicles between 9am and 4pm. It was great to see Sam and Jade again, who'd had a long day travelling from Huddersfield by coach. They'd brought their friend Chris with them, a double-bass player who had a really cool instrument case that looked like a coffin with 'Fragile' stickers on it. Chris told me the bus driver at Huddersfield had refused to let him on the coach with it, and he'd had to get a train instead.

I helped Sam and crew get their tents set up, and after they'd had something to eat, we got our instruments out and played music until about midnight. Jade had a lovely soulful voice that complemented the double-bass, and I played some lead guitar on top of Sam's intricate finger-picking. Although they weren't a full-time band, they'd written and recorded an album of original songs about birds, and called themselves Band of Jays. It was beautiful music, and we were getting lots of applause from the campers who were appreciating the late-night serenade.

It was sunny again the next day, and after breakfast Band of Jays climbed aboard Bluebell for the drive into town, with Sam and Chris sitting in the back so they could rehearse on the way.

'So have you ever been in a milk float before?' I asked Jade as we set off.

'Funnily enough it's my first time!' she replied.

Giving performers a lift into town in Bluebell was quickly becoming part of the 'Edinburgh experience'. Jade and I laughed most of the way in, which made the terrors of city driving much more bearable. When we arrived in town, I called into the Essential Edinburgh office to pick up my parking permit, and Brian introduced me to the other members of staff who he said would help me out if I had any problems over the next two weeks. After parking Bluebell on Castle Street, I went for a wander around Edinburgh to have a look at some of the Fringe events. The Royal Mile is where most of the action is happening, a cacophony of sight and sound, with lots of living statues (the best I saw was a wizard suspended in mid-air whose body looked like tree roots), theatre companies doing snippets of plays (MacBeth in a Minute), and people handing out flyers for all sorts of shows.

The Edinburgh Festival Fringe first began in 1947, when a group of eight theatre companies turned up unannounced at the Edinburgh International Festival. Taking advantage of the established crowds at the International Festival, they put on their shows on the streets and anywhere they could find that would host them. The theatre companies returned again the following year, when the term Edinburgh Fringe was coined by a local journalist and playwright, Robert Kemp, who wrote 'Round the fringe of official festival drama, there seems to be more private enterprise than before, I am afraid some of us are not going to be home during the evenings!'

The theatre companies kept returning and slowly the Fringe grew, with students from Edinburgh University organising beds and food at the local YMCA for performers, and in 1959 the Festival Fringe Society was formed. It has a written constitution of not vetting or censoring shows, and to this day anybody is able to come and perform at the Fringe, which is part of what makes it so exciting. In 2014 over 2,000,000 tickets were sold for almost 50,000 performances at 250 venues around the city, making it the largest arts festival in the world. Although initiated as a theatre fringe festival, it has grown to include musicals and opera, comedy, poetry and spoken word, music, art, and now of course milk floats!

I felt quite nervous as I set up my speakers and started my

first Fringe performance, but I soon had a good crowd gathered round, and Tanya, the organiser of the market, came over to say how nice the music sounded. Next up were Band of Jays, who did a lovely set, although it was quite a challenge getting Chris's double-bass to sound loud enough, as I had to plug it into my small guitar amplifier. While they were playing, Berney and Michaela from Ethemia arrived. It was the first time we'd met, but we'd been emailing a lot over the last few months, and they'd been spreading the word about my tour on social media.

Berney was a full-time guitar teacher in his 60s who had the enthusiasm of a 20 year-old, and Michaela had an equal zest for life, which combined made them a real tour de force. They'd been playing together as a duo for the last four or five years, and had been steadily growing their fan-base with appearances at festivals and on BBC Introducing. Ethemia's trademark was to hug everybody they possibly could, and they were soon spreading the love on the streets of Edinburgh. They had a great way of talking to the audience, involving them in the stories behind their songs, and of course giving them a hug or two.

The market was ending by the time Ethemia finished their set, and I drove back to the campsite before the rush hour traffic got too busy. I had a quiet night reflecting on how the first day at the Fringe had gone. Overall, I thought it had been a success, although I still felt I could do more to get some publicity for the Milk Float Stage. There are so many acts competing for space at the Fringe that you really have to sell yourself to get noticed, and thanks to the encouragement of

Michaela and Berney, that's exactly what was about to happen the next day.

A city of tents had sprung up next to me overnight on the campsite, and I soon got chatting to one of the performers, whose parents it turned out lived in the next village to mine in Norfolk. Jo was part of a choir based in Bristol that were collaborating with two other choirs from different parts of the country, to perform in a new musical called 'Hug!'. I couldn't wait to tell Michaela and Berney, who'd probably want to take part in the show given half a chance. I listened to the choirs rehearsing in the big marquee tent that had been erected on site as a make-shift cafe, and they sounded absolutely fantastic.

About mid-day Band of Jays climbed aboard Bluebell for another musical mystery tour into Edinburgh. There was a big weekend crowd at the market, and we all did well busking and selling CDs. While I was packing away, I got chatting to Michaela and Berney about an idea I'd had to get some publicity for the Milk Float Stage. I'd been watching a highlights programme of the Fringe on STV Edinburgh every night, and I thought I recognised the outdoor cafe that they filmed from, which was near to Haymarket Station.

'Do you fancy going on a mission to see if we can get on TV?' I said, to which Michaela and Berney replied in unison with an unequivocal 'Yes!'

Somehow, we managed to squeeze Michaela and Berney's guitars in the back of Bluebell, which was already piled up with my own and Band of Jay's instruments. Michaela climbed in the back, and I asked Berney if he'd help with directions. We were soon near Haymarket Station driving past the building where I thought STV filmed from, but it was a busy one-way street and there was nowhere to park.

'What about in there?' said Berney, pointing at a car park that had a big sign above it advertising a show called 'Ladyboys'.

I pulled off the road and ran up to the box office, explaining about my quest to get on TV. The guy at the box office went off to check with his manager, and came back to say it would be ok to park there for a while. I let Michaela out of the back of Bluebell, who'd been wondering why we'd pulled into a show called 'Ladyboys!'

'It was Berney's idea!', I joked as we set off for the studios.

We found the building that I thought STV were filming from, and sure enough there was a courtyard cafe at the back where a crowd were gathered ready for the show to start. I recognised the two presenters, who were sitting surrounded by cameramen and make-up artists.

'Now's your chance!' said Berney as we stood watching them. 'Go for it!' said Michaela.

I took a deep breath and went up to a man standing next to one of the cameramen, and said, 'Hi, I'm a musician and have travelled all the way from Norfolk in a milk float to play at the Fringe. Would there be any chance of talking to somebody about appearing on the show?'

'Yes, this man here,' he replied, pointing to the guy standing next to him. 'He's the producer.'

'So what's the highlight been so far?' Moray the producer asked me, after I'd explained to him about the tour. I paused for a moment, as there'd been so many special things that had happened it was hard to pick just one highlight out.

'Well, playing on the some of the islands like Colonsay was incredible,' I told him, 'Although driving to Ben Nevis in a milk float and then climbing up it on my birthday was hard to beat. I just love Scotland.'

'I think it's fantastic,' Moray said. 'Look, we're about to start filming, but can you give me your card and I'll be in touch on Monday about doing a feature.'

Michaela and Berney gave me a big hug and said, 'Well done, you were brilliant!'. After giving them a lift back to the Park and Ride, we stood chatting for a while about our respective musical paths. It's tough being an independent musician, as there is no financial certainty, and it can be lonely and overwhelming at times. But the more I spoke to the other acts on my tour, the more I came to understand that it's something we all feel compelled to do – it was music or nothing, and without it our lives would be incomplete.

EIGHTEEN

Turn It Down Please!

AFTER ANOTHER GIG in town the next day, I said goodbye to Michaela and Berney, who were driving back to Gloucestershire. I gave Band of Jays a lift back to the campsite as we were playing again that night in the marquee tent on-site, and was cooked a lovely vegetable curry by Sam, Jade and Chris, who made use of the pop-up kitchen, which supplied camping stoves, pots and pans for £1 a go. The music didn't start until late, as most of the people staying on the campsite were in town either watching or taking part in shows until about 10pm. Band of Jays warmed things up nicely, and I had a packed audience to play for. It was about 2am by the time I finished, and I couldn't get to sleep as it was pouring with rain, pounding off Bluebell's roof.

Band of Jays had packed their tents up and were sitting outside the marquee having breakfast when I finally surfaced the next day. Chris and Jade were travelling back to Huddersfield, and Sam was going to do some exploring around Scotland for the week. It had been a fun-filled few days together, and I would miss them. When the taxi arrived to take them into Edinburgh, I watched with amusement as they squeezed their tents, guitars and double-bass into the taxi.

After waving goodbye, I packed Bluebell up for another day of music. I had Edinburgh singer-songwriter Carrie MacDonald performing, as well as a very good singer-songwriter from Stroud called Hattie Briggs, who'd been getting played on national radio and had been nominated for the Radio Two Young Folk Musician of the Year award. Hattie's mum was a friend of Ethemia's, and had asked me the previous day if there would be any chance of Hattie playing, who was in town for a few days.

I was feeling tired from my late-night gig, and decided to take a day off playing, sitting in the back of Bluebell instead to enjoy listening to the other acts. Carrie wrote her own songs, which were powerful acoustic blues tunes, and Hattie played some beautiful folk songs of her own as well as a few covers by artists like Eva Cassidy and James Taylor. Hattie was halfway through a song, when a man with a posh English accent came up to her and said, 'You're not meant to be here, your permit says it's for George Street, not Castle Street.' When I asked him who he was, he said he was a local councillor, although he couldn't show me any ID. After arguing for almost ten minutes, he eventually disappeared muttering, 'We have laws to stop people like you from being here.'

I suspected that he'd be making a complaint the next day to Essential Edinburgh, which might mean having to move to a different spot. Tanya had said that I could play the following Wednesday at Waverley train station, where she ran another market once a week, and I still had several options of places to play on George Street. Thankfully, Hattie was able to finish the rest of her set in peace, and had a good crowd sitting outside the cafe opposite. I made my way back to the campsite afterwards, as I had Steve Young arriving that evening. He had a long drive from Hertfordshire, and had been having second thoughts about coming, as he'd seen a weather forecast predicting lots of rain over the coming days. I'd texted him to re-assure him that the campsite hadn't become a quagmire quite yet, and I wanted to be there when he arrived.

Steve had a lot of music equipment with him, and we persuaded Geoff and Rhyanne to let him park next to his tent, as somebody's car had been stolen from the car park at the front of the campsite the previous night. It turned out that Steve's worries about camping were mainly due to having never put a tent up before, and once we'd got pitched for the night, he seemed much happier. We walked to the local Co-op to buy some supplies and then got a BBQ going when we returned, sitting outside until late playing guitar.

Steve, myself, and Mikey from Perth were playing the Milk Float Stage the next day, and Steve and I headed into town late morning to set up. Steve made me laugh on the way in, because he kept complaining after every bump we went over with Bluebell. I'd become used to the poor suspension after so many miles of travelling, but for anyone having a ride in Bluebell for the first time it could be a little uncomfortable. I decided to carry on playing at Castle Street until I heard anything to the contrary from Essential Edinburgh, but we moved further down the street, where a hotdog seller had suggested we might do better now that the market was gone.

I'd been playing for about half an hour, when a guy from

one of the nearby office blocks came up to me and said, 'Can you turn it down please. It's annoying!' I'd been warned by Brian at Essential Edinburgh that we might get noise complaints, but it was only gentle acoustic music we were playing, and I couldn't imagine anyone would be able to even hear the music from the offices. I turned the volume down anyway, and finished my set off before Steve started playing. Not long after, I got a phone call from Moray, the producer at STV Edinburgh, who said one of his reporters would be along shortly to film and interview me. Meanwhile Mairi and Mikey had turned up, and I asked Mikey if he'd mind waiting to play until my interview was over, as we were going to be filming me playing a song, and I wanted to warm up before the reporter arrived.

'So what's it been like living in a milk float for the last two months?' Blare, the reporter from STV, asked me.

'Most of the time it's great,' I replied, 'although it does get cramped sometimes.'

I showed Blare the inside of Bluebell, which had guitar cases everywhere piled up amongst sandwich wrappers, discarded coffee cups, guitar leads and clothes. I really should have tidied up before my appearance on TV!

'What have been the highs and lows of the tour?' Blare asked me as I was showing him round Bluebell.

'The thing that's amazed me most, is just how untouched many parts of Britain still are,' I replied. 'It's really reassuring that you can travel for miles and miles without seeing another house or car…and travelling at the speed I'm doing has allowed me to appreciate my surroundings, although it does feel like I'm doing a marathon sometimes, and can get very tiring.'

I had a good crowd gathered round by the time I played my song 'Flights of Geese', which Blare asked me to perform a couple of times so that he could get all the shots he wanted. He said that the feature would be going out the next night on the STV Edinburgh Fringe Highlights show, and hopefully on national STV the following week. After listening to Mikey play a fantastic set of his own songs, we all went to Weatherspoons to celebrate our busking success and my new-found TV fame.

There was just Steve and me performing the next day, and we took it in turns playing for the afternoon, but my takings from busking that day were pitiful. I was still trying to figure out how I was going to get home, as cash was becoming tighter by the day. I couldn't believe it when I got a phone call that afternoon from my care agency, asking if I'd be available for a week's work in Edinburgh the following Tuesday. The timing was perfect, as I was finishing at the Fringe on Monday. I explained to the care manager about having the milk float with me, which he said he'd check would be ok with the elderly gentleman I'd be looking after, and half an hour later I had a phone call to say it was fine, and that the placement was arranged.

Meanwhile Steve had received another noise complaint from the same man as the previous day, and not long afterwards the police turned up. After promising to turn the music down, Steve finished his set and we packed up for the day, as it had become very windy, and I wanted to get back to the campsite in plenty of time to watch my feature on TV. Steve was going into town to watch some shows, and said that the next night he was determined to drag me along with him.

Back at camp, I had a cup of tea and some chocolate cake, ready to celebrate my TV appearance. About 15 minutes into the show, the presenter said, 'Now, the next act should probably get an award for the most unconventional form of travel ever to arrive at the Fringe. It's taken singer-songwriter Paul Thompson over two months to get here in a milk float…oh, and he stopped off at the Outer Hebrides and Ben Nevis on the way!' The feature cut to me standing outside Bluebell singing 'Flights of Geese' with a lovely shot of the castle in the background, and then interspersed the interview with my music. The piece went on for over five minutes, and I couldn't believe that they'd given me so much air-time. I just hoped that the extra publicity would help to boost interest in The Milk Float Stage over the coming days.

The next morning Johnny Steinberg turned up, a singer-songwriter from Norfolk. Johnny was in his mid-50s, and had come to song writing late in life. I'd liked the tracks he'd sent me a link to when he applied to play at the Fringe, and it turned out that we'd both written a song called 'Man On Wire' about the French tight-rope walker Phillipe Petit, who walked across the Twin Towers on a tightrope in the 1970s. After introducing Johnny to Steve, we piled our guitars into the back of Bluebell (we now had six guitars and a ukelele!), and Johnny took his turn in the front cab for the ritual drive into town. Even after all this time, it still made me chuckle at the wackiness of travelling by milk float, which was made fresh again by having new people aboard.

'You do realise you're absolutely bonkers don't you?', said Johnny, as we turned out of the airport onto the A8.

'Thanks a lot, I'll take that as a compliment,' I replied.

It was really windy again, and I felt sorry for Johnny, who was busking for the first time. The wind kept blowing his music stand over and banging his guitar case shut, making it difficult for passers-by to give money.

'Is busking always this hard?' Johnny asked afterwards, who I think was beginning to wonder whether the trip all the way from Norfolk had been worth it.

We stopped off at a huge guitar shop on the way back to the campsite to cheer ourselves up, and I finally managed to get the pick-up fixed on my guitar. After a quick bite to eat, we caught a bus back into town. Many of the shows at the Fringe are free to get in, and after trying three or four stand-up comedy shows, we headed to a music bar called The Cow Shed that Steve had been to the night before. It was an underground car park that was transformed into a music venue during the Fringe, with saloon-style swinging doors at the entrance, and hay bales stacked around the tables. Johnny and Steve were getting into the festival spirit downing pints of beer, and I felt a little out of place as I was just about the only sober person in the building.

'So where do you want to go next?' Steve asked me.

'Is there somewhere outside we could go? It's a bit cramped in here!' I replied.

This made Steve and Johnny laugh, who thought I was getting withdrawal symptoms after spending too much time outdoors in the Milk Float Dimension. We went for a walk up to the castle, following tiny cobbled alleyways, and eventually found an Irish Bar with some lively music going on. It was the early hours of the morning by the time we caught a bus back to the airport, and we got chatting to a performance poet from Lowestoft, who was staying at the campsite. We sat at the back of the bus for the half-hour journey, with me telling the story of my tour so far, and everyone agreed that it had been the most entertaining thing they'd heard all night.

The next morning, I said goodbye to Steve who had a gig to do that night in Hertfordshire, and Johnny and I headed back into town. Daria Kulesh turned up mid-afternoon to play a set, and it was great to catch up with each other's news. Daria said she couldn't play the following day as she had another gig to do, but would be joining me for the final three days of the Fringe. I was relieved to get packed away after our third day of struggling against the wind, and wasn't planning on returning to Castle Street to play. We'd be performing at Waverley Station the following day, and I wanted to try my luck further up George Street during the weekend to see if we could attract a bigger crowd.

Johnny navigated for me on our way to Waverley Station the next morning, which is just off Waverley bridge in the centre of Edinburgh. Tanya had given me instructions, saying that I'd need to buzz in at the barrier, and that an attendant would let me through.

'Ah, the milk float man. I've been expecting you!', the attendant said when we arrived. We were soon in a subterranean world of trains, and Tanya guided me into the entrance of the station where the market was being set up. It wasn't an ideal spot, as we were parked next to a tannoy that would suddenly announce things like, 'The train approaching platform six is the 11.52 arrival from Dundee.' To make matters worse, a bag-piper turned up and started playing just yards from us. If you've ever tried competing to be heard above the noise of a bag-piper, let's just say it's not an equal competition. I stood waiting until the man had finished playing a tune, and then said, 'Excuse me, do you have permission to be here?' to which he replied, 'Yes, I'm waiting for the Flying Scotsman.'

After some discussion, the piper explained that he'd been booked to play by the train company to greet passengers off the famous steam train when it stopped off on its journey up to the Highlands. The man, who was dressed in full traditional costume, went on to tell me that the train would be full of millionaires, and that he himself was a millionaire. I'd obviously chosen the wrong instrument for busking, as I'd only made about £2 so far that day!

Meanwhile Johnny finished playing his set, and said, 'I think I've just about given up the will to live!' I knew exactly what he meant, and we consoled ourselves with some burgers that one of the market stall holders had kindly given us, munching them whilst we watched the millionaires parade off the train onto a red carpet that had been laid down for them. Tanya told me that the Queen was coming on the royal train the following week, and I thought it was a pity that I couldn't be there to offer her a lift in Bluebell. But I had better things to do, and after thanking Tanya for inviting us to play, we made a sharp exit from the station. I drove back to the campsite on my own, as Johnny was going into town to watch some more shows, and I had my brother Dave and family arriving from Aberdeen.

The next morning, I waved goodbye to Johnny as he set off on the long journey back to Norfolk, and I drove into town with Dave and Anne in the back of Bluebell, with Anna sitting in the front cab, joined of course by her favourite teddy bear Polar. I found a spot about halfway up George Street that had plenty of room for Bluebell to park alongside the pavement, opposite a couple of independent clothes shops. As I was setting up my music gear, the manager of one of the shops came out and said, 'Excuse me, could you keep the noise down?'

This wasn't a good start, as I hadn't even played a note yet! I explained that I had permission to perform on George Street, to which the man replied that he was paying rent for his shop, and didn't see why I should be able to just turn up unannounced. Eventually I placated him by pointing my speakers well away from his shop entrance, and after playing a couple of songs he came out and put his thumbs up to say thank you. Meanwhile, the owner of the other clothes shop where the speakers were now pointing towards was staring daggers at me, despite her customers obviously enjoying the music, as they were putting money in my guitar case as they went in and out of the shop.

After about half an hour the shop owner came out and said, 'I can't hear my customers. Can you turn it down?' If I'd turned the speakers down any more I wouldn't have been able to hear myself, so I told the woman I'd point the speakers away from the shop, and directed them towards The Assembly Rooms, where a crowd of people were lining up to see a show.

Despite getting rounds of applause from the queuing Assembly Room punters, it wasn't long before a lady from the box office came over and said, 'I'm ever so sorry, one of the performers has made a noise complaint. He's a bit awkward, to be honest, but could you turn it down?'

I had no choice but to comply, although my set was almost finished, and it was poor Daria who had to struggle to be heard above the noise of the busy Saturday street. She did a fantastic job of attracting a crowd by doing some traditional folk tunes and dances, singing in Russian as well as English. I went off with Dave, Anne and Anna to watch some of the street entertainment, and when we got back Daria said she'd received another noise complaint. The constant struggle against irate shopkeepers and office workers was really starting to get me down, and we decided to call it a day.

The drive back to the campsite was interesting to say the least, as Scotland had been playing a rugby match against Italy in the World Cup at Twickenham, and the crowd was coming out of the stadium as I drove past Haymarket Station. The Scottish fans were in the middle of the road singing at the tops of their voices and waving flags, and when they spotted Bluebell they started cheering even louder, banging on the side as I drove past. I just hoped that nobody would try and climb in the cab, but luckily I escaped onto the A8, where I soon had a massive queue of traffic behind me as the Saturday shoppers and rugby fans tried to make their way home.

The next day I drove into town and found a different place to park on George Street, just outside Weatherspoons. It was a much better spot, and we had a good crowd gathered round, with festival goers and drinkers from the pub cheering us on. Daria and I went for a walk afterwards up Arthur's Seat, the big hill that overlooks Edinburgh, and sat for a while gazing across the city. It was strange thinking that the next day would be the final day of performing on my tour. I wasn't planning on playing any music on my way back to Norfolk as I needed a break, and wanted to enjoy the journey without worrying about deadlines. I'd worked out a route down the east side of the country, crossing over the border into England near Berwick-on-Tweed, then following the coastline from Lindisfarne around Newcastle, past Whitby towards the Humber Bridge and finally home. I didn't want any more breakdowns, and had mapped the flattest route I could, although I had a feeling that the Milk Float Dimension still had one or two surprises for us along the way.

NINETEEN

Homeward Bound

I PARKED BLUEBELL outside Weatherspoons again the next day, but despite it being a Bank Holiday Monday, the city had a very different feel with barely any people around except for a few office workers and shoppers. After playing for an hour I'd only made £5, and my heart just wasn't in being there. It was a disappointing way to end the tour, but Daria was lovely when I said I was feeling a bit low, and she told me how much I'd inspired her and many other people by doing my journey. We went for some tea and cake to celebrate our last day at Edinburgh, and gave each other a farewell hug.

When I got back to the campsite, all the rows of performer tents had been packed down, revealing bare patches of brown grass where they'd been pitched for the last month. Geoff and Rhyanne were cooking for all the crew, and offered me some food, giving me a huge helping of sausages and mashed swede with onion gravy. I thanked everyone for making me so welcome, providing such a safe haven during my time at the Fringe.

I had to find my way around the busy Edinburgh ring road the next morning on the way to my care work placement, with fast-moving vehicles flying past us on four-lane highways. Eventually I turned onto a quieter B-road that led towards a wealthy-looking housing estate where I'd be staying for the next week. Mr P. was a lovely old gentleman in his 90s, who thought it was marvellous that I'd travelled all the way from Norfolk in a milk float. Despite some inquisitive looks from the neighbours, I kept Bluebell parked on the road outside his house for the next week, using her to go shopping at the local supermarket, and running any errands that Mr P. wanted doing.

In his working life, Mr P. had been a lecturer, and had spent his long holidays travelling the world. We had an interesting week telling each about the different places we'd visited, and Mr P. also had a massive record collection which we waded through. We debated philosophy, religion and politics, and I hoped that if lived to be Mr P.'s age I'd still be as open-minded as he was. During my afternoon breaks, I planned my route home in more detail. I was having problems finding anywhere to camp around the Newcastle area, as I'd be there during the weekend of the Great North Run. My only other option would be to go back towards Hadrian's Wall, which I wanted to avoid if I possibly could. I worked out that I should be able to get home in about two weeks if I did at least 30 miles per day, and the thought of getting back to my creature comforts was becoming ever more appealing.

I left Mr P.'s one foggy Tuesday evening on the long journey home. The nights were really drawing in, and it was freezing cold as I drove round the Edinburgh ring road onto the A7, stuck in the tail-end of rush-hour traffic. I had an orange beacon flashing on the back of bluebell to warn other drivers that I was a slow-moving vehicle, but even so it was a dangerous situation as the cars overtaking me couldn't see what was coming the other way. I had about 22 miles to travel to my campsite, at a place called Carfraemill, and the last few miles were almost all uphill on the busy A68, with visibility reduced to about 50 yards. My campsite was next to a pub just off the A68, and after eventually finding my turning and getting pitched up for the night, I went for a meal to warm up.

The next morning spiderwebs hung from Bluebell's wing-mirrors, decorated with dew in the early autumn mist. The sun soon cleared the mist away as I drove towards Coldstream on a beautiful road lined with stone walls and fox-gloves, surrounded by wide undulating hills full of cattle and sheep. I stopped at a place called Greenlaw to let Bluebell cool down, and I could see the hills of England in the distance with huge shafts of light pouring onto them. I had shivers running down my spine as I stood watching them, feeling that somehow I was being welcomed home. After Greenlaw, I turned off towards Norham, where we crossed over into Northumberland. I had a quiet night on the campsite of a lovely old pub called The Plough Inn, at a place called West Allerdean. I was only about 15 miles from Lindisfarne, and worked out that if I set off early the next morning, I could drive across the causeway to visit the island while the tide was still out.

There was thick dew on the ground again when I woke up the next day, and the pub looked beautiful with its thatched roof and corn-fields behind. I set off in Bluebell through the wilds of Northumberland, singing as I went, passing farms in the middle of nowhere with barely any traffic on the narrow, winding roads. It was a bit of a culture shock when I turned onto the A1 and suddenly had huge lorries thundering past, but I only had two miles to travel before turning off again onto a quiet road that led to the Lindisfarne causeway. The crossing times to Lindisfarne vary by an hour each day according to the tides, with roughly a six-hour window when it's safe to cross. I followed a hilly road for about four miles to the entrance of the causeway, and stopped to take some photos of Bluebell next to a sign that said, 'Danger. Do not proceed when water reaches causeway.' It was a spectacular crossing, with the blue sky and billowing clouds reflected in the mud flats, and the ancient castle of Holy Island rising across the causeway.

The first recorded history of Lindisfarne dates back to the 6th Century, when a priory was founded by the Irish monk Saint Aiden. The island became well known for its beautiful Celtic artwork, most notably the Lindisfarne Gospels, as well as the production of mead. One of the earliest Viking raids in Britain was carried out on Lindisfarne in 793, and by the end of the 9th Century the monks had all fled. The priory was re-established in Norman Times, when the island became known as Holy Island, named after saints Aiden and Cuthbert. In 1536 the priory was dissolved by Henry VIII, and in more recent times the islanders made a living from fishing and lime production.

Today there are around 180 full-time inhabitants on the island, which stretches just 1.5 miles from north to south, and three miles from east to west. Vehicles aren't allowed into the village, and a huge car park full of tourist coaches stands at the entrance. The shops were full of 'holy' gifts, and the ruins of the priory were packed with people taking photos. I couldn't help but feel disappointed that what was meant to be a sacred place was so geared up towards tourism. After walking away from the village to the castle, I found a lovely stone walled garden full of sweet peas in bloom, and sat for a while breathing in their fragrance and enjoying the autumn sunshine, contemplating what life on the island would have been like in days gone by.

I crossed back over the causeway before the tide came back in, which strands about one vehicle per month that has to be rescued by either the RNLI lifeboat from Seahouses, or an RAF helicopter. I can't imagine the RAF would have been too impressed by a guy stuck in a three-ton milk float, standing on top frantically waving a guitar at them! After driving back onto the A1, I had another six miles to go before my turning towards Bamburgh, with a stream of cars and lorries overtaking all the way.

Bamburgh has the most impressive castle I'd seen on my tour so far, a wide, imposing fortress standing on cliffs overlooking the sea. I followed the coast road to Seahouses, and drove the remaining ten miles or so to my campsite at Dunstan Steads with the battery meter flashing red. Bluebell travelled 41 miles that day, equalling our record for long-distance travel. As usual it wasn't battery power but milk that I ran out of when I finally reached the camp site. The staff at Dunstan Steads Camping and Caravan Site were really friendly, and after purchasing a pint of milk from their shop, we took some photos with Bluebell that they wanted to send off to the Camping and Caravanning Club magazine. After getting Bluebell on charge, I went for a long walk along the sand dunes to the remains of

Dunstanburgh Castle, and sat watching the sun set over Lindisfarne.

The next morning, I continued on the coast road past miles of sand dunes and remote farms, until reaching the A1068 at Alnmouth. It was a much busier road than I'd expected, and I changed my planned route, turning off by Warkworth Castle instead, following a quieter B-road towards a place called Widdrington. I stopped at a Spar shop in South Broomhill to get some supplies, and got chatting to the cashier, who it turned out had lived on Benbecula, where I'd passed through in the Outer Hebrides. It would have been rude not to show the lady around Bluebell, and we spent another quarter of an hour chatting out in the car park as she told me more about growing-up on Benbeula.

I was staying that night at a campsite called Blue Sky Equestrian Centre, at Linton, about 20 miles above Newcastle, which turned out to be a horse-riding school with a camping field attached. Christine, the owner, had done a fantastic job converting a barn into 'The Blue Sky Blues Bar', and she asked if I'd play a few songs for the campers later on. I spent the afternoon phoning round campsites to try and book somewhere to stay the following night, but everywhere was full except for a farm at a place called Newton, just above Hadrian's Wall.

It would be a risk going that way, as once I'd got past Hadrian's Wall, I'd be driving on the hilliest section of the A68, which I'd avoided on my way to Scotland by crossing the north Pennines instead. My only other option would have been to stay put for the weekend, which would have meant another two or three days of travelling time lost. I decided to risk the hilly route, and booked onto the campsite at Newton, hoping that Bluebell would be better equipped to climb the hills now that her motor had been re-built. I had a nice night in The Blue Sky Blues Bar, playing songs and chatting with the campers. Christine got a huge fire going in the hearth, and supplied me with plenty of hot-chocolate to keep the autumn chills at bay. I made friends with a guy from Newcastle called Geordie who was pitched in a caravan next to me, and he said he'd treat me to breakfast the next day in Ashington, the nearest town.

It was cold and wet in the morning when we set off, but I was in no rush to leave as I only had about 25 miles to drive that day, and was hoping the weather might clear by the afternoon. Geordie took me to a Weatherspoons in Ashington that was serving breakfast, and I couldn't believe how many people were drinking beer at 10 o'clock in the morning. Geordie insisted on paying for my breakfast, and after getting some supplies for my journey ahead, we went back to his caravan for another cup of tea. It was still raining when I left at mid-day, following a quiet cross-country route that was fairly flat. The campsite I was staying on at Newton was waterlogged from all the rain, and after skidding around on the field for a while, I eventually managed to pitch up and get Bluebell on charge. There wasn't much I could do for the rest of the day due to the weather, so I climbed in my sleeping-bag and stayed there watching my little TV.

I was on the road again by 7am the next morning in lovely autumn sunshine, and drove down a huge hill that wound for almost two miles to the start of the A68. It was a good job nothing was coming the other way, as there were no passing places, and the road was barely wide enough for Bluebell, her wing-mirrors grazing the sides of bramble hedges as we sped our way down. The view was spectacular, though, and I could see past Hadrian's Wall to the hills of the North Pennines. Apart from the occasional lorry, there was no traffic on the A68, but after doing only four miles of steep hills I realised there was no way we were going to get to our planned destination. I'd booked onto a campsite 25 miles away, but the battery meter had already dropped below half, and I could smell burning coming from Bluebell's motor. We crawled to the top of a hill which had a crossroads with a lay-by next to it, and I pulled over to let Bluebell cool down.

We still had the steepest section of the A68 to come at Castleside, by which time there would be a lot more traffic about, and it could be quite dangerous. I was fairly sure if I carried on, I'd burn Bluebell's motor out again, and I couldn't bear the thought of returning to Norfolk on the back of a lorry when we were so close to completing our mission. I phoned the AA and asked to be taken by lorry to Thirsk, where I'd planned to reach the following day. The road flattened out after Thirsk on the way to York, and we should be pretty much home and dry.

Half an hour later a friendly AA man called Gary turned up in a huge lorry, and he soon had Bluebell loaded on the back. As we drove over Castleside, I felt a massive sense of relief that I'd phoned for help, as the road was incredibly steep and long, and would almost certainly have spelt the end of the tour. It took us about an hour and a half to reach Thirsk Racecourse, where I was booked onto a Caravan Club Site for the night. After unloading Bluebell, I went for a wander round

Thirsk, which is a lovely old town full of historic buildings. I spent the evening with my map working out the rest of my route home, which all being well would get me back to Norfolk in six days.

It was freezing cold and wet when I set off for York the next day, and I had to put on two jumpers beneath my coat to keep warm, as well as wearing woolly socks, a hat and gloves. I drove for almost 20 miles along the A19 towards York, with one vehicle after another overtaking us, but the road was fairly straight and wide, allowing the traffic to get past easily enough. I wanted to stop to look round York, but after driving through the centre I couldn't find anywhere to park. Eventually I reached a massive shopping complex on the outskirts that had a Park and Ride, and I left Bluebell and caught a bus into town. York reminded me a lot of Norwich, with its castle and battlements still largely intact, and narrow cobbled streets leading to the cathedral. I spent a while gazing up at the stone carvings of gargoyles on the outer walls of the cathedral, and afterwards went for a walk through The Shambles, which claims to be the oldest shopping street in Europe.

I wanted to reach my campsite before it got dark, and caught a bus back to the Park and Ride, hoping to beat the rush-hour traffic. After taking one look inside the shopping-complex at the Park and Ride, I turned straight round and walked out again. It looked so ugly and unnatural after all my time spent in the Milk Float Dimension, and I was glad to reach the safety of my campsite on a farm at Escrick, which had a huge conker tree in the middle of the field. I was the only person there, and after cooking supper I spent the night in my sleeping bag playing guitar, listening to the wind knocking conkers off the tree onto Bluebell's roof.

I couldn't help but laugh when I set off the next morning, and spotted a horsebox on the A19 being towed by a taxi. I wondered if the two horses in the back of the horsebox had ordered the taxi.

'Hello, I'd like a taxi to take my friend and I to the races at York please…Yes, the name's Mr Ed. Do you accept credit-card payments?'

After distracting myself for a while with imaginary conversations between upwardly mobile horses, I got fed up with all the traffic and turned off the A19 onto a quieter road towards a place called Howden, which took me onto the A63. I had a terrifying 10 miles or so driving the final section towards the Humber Bridge, and in the end stopped looking in the rear mirror, feeling a bit like a tight-rope walker who mustn't look down, concentrating instead on what was ahead. As I drove up to the toll booth at the entrance to the Humber Bridge I shouted, 'Good girl Bluebell, you've done it!'. We'd crossed the worst of the hills, and had more or less finished with A-roads. I felt on a real high as I crossed the Humber Bridge for the second time on my journey, and after finding my campsite I went into town to treat myself to some fish and chips to celebrate being another step closer to home.

I had 40 miles to travel the next day to Saltfeet, a small coastal village about 15 miles below Grimsby. I wanted to steer well clear of the Lincolnshire Wolds, having broken down there at Scramblesby Hill back in June, and although the scenery wasn't as interesting the way we were going, it was almost completely flat, which meant Bluebell could travel much further each day. You know that you're in the slow lane when even tractors overtake you, and I had an impatient tractor driver following me for almost two miles on the way to a place called Waltham, just past Grimsby. When he finally overtook, the tractor driver pulled in deliberately close to me so that his trailer almost caught Bluebell's front wheel-arch, and stuck his fingers up at me as he drove off. I wasn't going to let anything spoil my day, though, and I sang the rest of the way to Saltfleet, enjoying the understated beauty of the grassy sand dunes that led to the sea far away in the distance.

It poured with rain overnight, but was lovely and sunny again the next morning as I set off for Wrangle Bank, just above The Wash. After stopping at the pretty town of Alford for some lunch, I drove through the villages of Welton Le Marsh and Irby in the Marsh, following a maze of flat fields with open sky stretching in all directions. My campsite at Wrangle Bank was part of a farm that had a few pitches at the end of a track, divided by willow hedges full of wasps. After parking up I got chatting to another camper who said the wasps disappeared at night time, and once I'd got Bluebell on charge, I climbed back inside as quickly as I could, not daring to come out again until it was dark. My forced internment in Bluebell helped me to start writing a new song called 'A Little Piece of Heaven', about coming home. The wasps were well and truly tucked up in bed by the time I walked down to the campsite loos to brush my teeth. There was a lovely stillness in the air with a fresh smell of autumn, and I stood watching the stars for a while, which were ablaze beneath the dark and silent fens.

The next day I followed a huge dyke along a straight and narrow road called Hobhole Bank, that came out just before Boston. I stopped in the town to pick up a few supplies, and after driving for about a mile on the A16, turned off into the flatlands again. The roads were a continual maze of farmland, and if it hadn't been for the satnav I would have been totally lost. I'd worked out a route that took me to Fosdyke Bridge, where the A17 crosses the River Welland, the only place I could get over the river. There was a turning just past the bridge that would get me immediately off the A17, which was a good job as I was only on the road for about five minutes, and already had a huge tailback of lorries stuck behind Bluebell.

My campsite for the night was in the grounds of a pub called The Rose and Crown at Holbeach Hurn, and it got confusing as we passed Holbeach Saint Marks and then Holbeach Saint Matthew on the way, ignoring the signs for Holbeach and Holbeach Bank as we neared our destination. Our 32 miles of travelling that day had taken us right around the Wash, and the next day I'd be crossing the county border into Norfolk. I made the most of the September sunshine, sitting outside reading for the afternoon, and later on treated myself to a meal in the pub.

It was sunny again the next morning as I set off for King's Lynn, with a longer section of the A17 to travel on just past Sutton Bridge, where the main road crosses the River Nene. I'd definitely done the right thing leaving early, as even at 8 o'clock Bluebell had a queue of lorries behind her. My heart jumped for joy as we passed the border sign for Norfolk, and turned off the main road again, travelling on the old King's Lynn road towards the River Ouse. The people of King's Lynn must have wondered what was going on as I drove through the city centre and out again the other side, singing the classic Muddy Waters song 'I've Got My Mojo Working' at the top of my voice, and tooting Bluebell's horn at random bystanders. I celebrated my arrival back in Norfolk by stopping at the village of Castle Rising, where the beautiful ruins of a medieval fortress stand on a hill overlooking the county.

After brewing up a cup of tea, I sat in the back of Bluebell finishing my elegy to Norfolk, 'A Little Piece of Heaven'. They say that absence makes the heart grow fonder, and I knew then where my heart truly belonged. I was planning on staying with my dad for a few days when I got back, and phoned him up to let him know I'd be there the following day. I still had another 60 miles to go, stopping the night at Hunstanton and then following the coast road home the next day, and I didn't want to count my blessings too early, as despite what people say about Norfolk being flat, I knew that the coast road was very hilly in places.

The road from Castle Rising to Hunstanton was a mass of caravans plodding along behind us for several miles, and at one point when I pulled over I counted more than 100 frustrated drivers passing us. It took almost 15 minutes to get out of the lay-by again, and after that I decided to just keep going until I reached Hunstanton. Needless to say, one of the biggest traffic jams in history was seen in Hunstanton that day, and I tried to look as innocent as I could as I pulled off the main road and drove towards the seafront, where I was booked onto a large caravan park. I spent the afternoon relaxing on the beach, treating myself to an ice cream and watching the holiday crowds come and go. It seemed an unreal world of roller-coasters and candy-floss, so far removed from the wilds of Scotland, but it was still home, and I wouldn't have wanted to be anywhere else.

I woke at 6am the next morning and pulled open Bluebell's curtains to reveal a perfect blue sky. An hour later I was driving away from Hunstanton with the North Sea sparkling in the autumn sunshine, and I sang the whole way home, passing the villages of Holkham, Burnham Market and Wells-Next-the-Sea. I pulled in at Blakeney harbour and bought a bacon roll from a food stall that was just opening, and sat in the back of Bluebell brewing a cup of tea and looking out at the small boats bobbing on the water. I was in exactly the same spot as I'd been on that May morning when I'd taken Bluebell on her first proper test-run, unsure of whether she could do a 30-mile round-trip, let alone travelling to the Outer Hebrides and back. Since then we'd survived a 1,500-mile journey at an average speed of 10mph, crossing oceans and mountain ranges, overcoming breakdowns and exhaustion, and generally causing a lot of traffic jams.

So what had I learnt from my time in the Milk Float Dimension? As I sat watching the boats, I thought about all the friends I'd made on my journey, often complete strangers who'd helped in my time of need for no other reason than to be kind. I realised that despite the pace of life we live at these days, people are still willing to find the time to help others. Being away from home for so long had also taught me how much I value friends and family. Deep down, I think we all long for the same things in life, to be surrounded by people we love, and to have a sense of belonging. Travelling by milk float had given me a rare and privileged opportunity to see Britain in a completely different light, truly appreciating an untouched and wild beauty in a landscape that I hadn't known still existed.

Months after returning from tour, it was finally confirmed by the Guinness World Records team that I was indeed the holder of the Guinness World Record for the 'Longest Journey by Electric Milk Float', officially measured at 1,031 miles. When I received my certificate, I remembered the words of the director of the dairy, who'd told me before I left, 'It would be a bloody miracle if I made it back in one piece.' Now that I'd completed my journey, I wanted to tell him just one thing.

I believe in miracles.

About the Author

Paul Thompson is a writer and musician from Norfolk, England. He has toured in the US, Canada and Europe, as well as around the British Isles in his mobile milk float stage 'Bluebell'.

Paul's 2015 *Floating to the Fringe Tour* gained him a Guinness World Record for 'the longest journey by electric milk float', and in 2017 Paul did another milk float tour, *Bluebell's Busking Bonanza*, from Norfolk to Land's End in Cornwall, raising money for Cancer Research.

After breaking down in Somerset on the return journey, Paul applied to do a Master's Degree in Songwriting at Bath Spa University, and remained in Somerset for a further year, recording his album *One Again* in a motorhome studio that was converted for him by *Sound on Sound* magazine.

Eventually returning to his Norfolk home, Paul continues to write, record, teach and produce music, as well as dreaming up quirky travel adventures. For all the latest information, and to listen to Paul's music, float over to his website, www.paulsmusic.co.uk.

Printed in Great Britain
by Amazon